An Insiders Secret: Mastering the Hollywood Path

Alexia Melocchi

DEDICATION & ACKNOWLEDGEMENTS

To my Mother, Alexandra, who taught me about the importance of class, integrity, and reaching for the stars.

Special Thanks to;
My wonderful editor Heidi, Debbie for keeping me connected to my heart, Susan for her no B.S advice, Maryam for inviting me to write for the Eden Magazine, Amanda and R.B for nudging me to teach what I know, all my podcast guests (you all showed me that artists out there are building new words with their work), Phoenix for reminding me what is possible, my grandmother Kiveli who showed me we can be stars of our world, Tony Robbins for taking massive action, my 3 cats Tutu, Cinnamon and Ferrari for teaching me to be present, my beloved cat Cairo who broke my heart open, my ex-husband for setting me free so I can go after my dreams, my clients (you know who you are) buyers, filmmakers, writers, authors, producers who have put their trust in me but most of all, again, to my mother who brought me to America-because that's when my life really started.

CONTENTS

TESTIMONIAL

From 10,000 ft, it is an incredibly smooth read and a wonderful blend of encouragement and truthism about the entertainment industry. A road map for implementation once you crack a door and a support system for the psyche after entering the room. It's also a training manual on how to react, move forward, learn, appreciate, and behave.

So many great bits of wisdom like, the value of your and/or the pro you work withs time. Or how important quality of work is. (Local commercials... so true)

And comparing your work to other projects might seem bankable to some when most movie goers hate predictability.

"Money is the byproduct of doing the right thing". Such an important truth. I like how the book ties that into pitching and marketing.

The extra chapter conversations with Jay, DeeDee, and Evan was the cherry on top.

Something I reflected on throughout... listen, listen, listen, speak a little bit, then listen.

Kelly Namey, Writer

HOW DID I GET HERE?

As a Hollywood producer and executive, and a fierce lover of visual images, I have gotten my hands dirty to protect and champion stories, and artists who stand out for something.

I have been fostering their talent, so that everything they created will make its way into the big or small screen.

I want to share with you a little snapshot of the path that I took which shaped my authentic way of being in Hollywood, through a collection of blogs and articles that I have released over the years to help pave the way for others on the same journey.

If you look at my movie credits, and I have over 30 movies in the can, and my social media feed, you would think that all has come effortlessly my way.

However, how many times have we seen artists go on stage and pick up Oscars and various awards, and then we get to hear their stories of years of personal struggle before success? I stand before you as a Hollywood producer, known for dedication to nurturing storytellers and promoting excellence in film and TV to remind you that my path to success was far from conventional.

I was born in Italy, and I arrived in America as a teenager, with only $5000 in my pocket (well, actually in my mother's pocket). And I had a big dream. My dream was to go to America and attend an American High School, and just be in Hollywood where all the stars and storytellers were. My story is one of resilience, I followed the courageous path of my mother, who left an unhappy marriage to bring me to the States, the land of opportunity, with determination to carve out a better life for her. For me, I would spend hours watching American shows and dreaming of moving to California to Los Angeles, a city that I had not even seen what it looked like in real life.

Because of my mother's bravery, who is also my business partner to this day, I am here. She is an example of integrity, values, dreaming big, and fierce determination. Through a series of magical events, show business found me.

In Tinseltown, I was meeting the stars and the creators of movies that I admired as a little girl in Italy. I became enamored with how I felt when I went to a movie that spoke not only to myself but to everyone watching it. I was willing to do whatever it took to be a part of that.

I started at the bottom, and I worked my way up. I worked in small production companies answering phones, vacuuming, learning everything by "paying my dues" and listening to those who had already made their life a success.

Even today, after decades in Hollywood, I keep on growing, and I keep on learning, showing empathy and kindness to everyone every step of the way, even to those who were not so kind to me.

My background is of an immigrant woman in a male-dominated industry. It is the context of a story. But it is not the story itself. My circumstances do not define me. I define myself. To this day, my mother's wisdom, which was shared with me on my first day in an American High School, as a foreigner in a foreign land still echoes in my mind. She said: It's not how others define you. It's how you define yourself.

So instead of allowing labels to confine me, as an immigrant, a woman, with no college degree to hang on the wall, but through the school of hard knocks, not Hollywood skinny, self-funded - I harnessed my superpower, which was my ability to connect and my integrity. And that is how I became a strong player in this industry, growing a lot as a person along the way.

I created a brand that reflected my true essence. I did not let societal perceptions limit me. I used the international routes, and my fluency in several languages as leverage. I amplified my entrepreneurial spirit, I took risks. I championed the underdogs in the arts, and all this to transform a mere $5,000 that I had with me when I first came to the United States into a million dollars in personal revenue by the age of 21.

We are in a world driven by numbers, statistics, degrees, and likes on Instagram. However, I chose to focus on my unique attributes and make them my superpower. In my pursuit of Hollywood success, I have failed, and I have succeeded. I have won, and I have lost many times. I've been in a realm of storytellers that does attract vultures and narcissists, the power-hungry.

I was determined to use my voice to protect the storytellers. And while I was helping others use their voices, at times, inevitably silenced my own. It's an irony many of us face. We empower those around us, but we forget to empower ourselves.

Sometimes you will also discover why what you thought was authentic was something that someone else told you should be. Or you may discover the lies you tell yourself. In the lies, lies your biggest truth. Think about Virgin without Branson, or Tesla without Elon Musk, those are iconic names, but behind them are individuals who dare to dream and very clearly communicate their visions. They have shown the world the genuine desire to make a difference and become trailblazers in their fields.

In the heart of show business, where stories do come alive, I found my mission to be a protector and a mentor to storytellers to bring people together to the magic of film and television from all over the world. My brand is the heartbeat of this world I have envisioned, and I believe that my heart will guide me to further heights of success.

These chapters are articles I have written for various Industry blogs and part of my observations as a speaker at top Industry events. Consider them cliff notes to give you some real insider information on how Hollywood truly works, from pitching to development to production to distribution and even actions you can take to become a creative leader and manage your time and mindset.

As a special bonus, I am adding a few chapters from my next book (keep a lookout!) where I have my podcast guests talk about different topics in show business, their transformative journeys, and what challenges they faced as they were making a name for themselves.

Enjoy these wisdom nuggets, and I hope you make your own as you make your move through Hollywood!

-Alexia

WHY YOUR REPUTATION IS MORE IMPORTANT THAN YOUR TALENT

There is no Business like Show Business.

And possibly that is true, as there is no place, other than politics, that a good or bad reputation can travel faster than a supersonic jet.

You have to treat your reputation as your most prized possession in Hollywood. There seems to be a misunderstanding about what reputation truly means. A solid reputation is built on professionalism but even more so on how good a human being you are on a solid ground of authenticity and I, for one, quote more than once the saying, "This is not Show Friends, it is Show Business," because there has to be a definite approach to a career in film and television by displaying the proper business etiquette.

Ultimate success is achieved with both talent and relationships, and this combination creates a positive reputation.

As Stage 32 CEO R.B Botto has spoken about so eloquently in my podcast, The Heart of Show Business, I want to remind you that "you are the CEO of YOU, INC".

You have to treat your career primarily as a business first, with a VITAL element of authentic networking and genuine relationships from the very beginning.

Connection and relationships trump talent every single time.

How often have you seen a writer, director, or actor who wasn't as talented as an A-Lister gain elite status because of close friendships with decision-makers?

How many times have you seen artists stand out from a crowd and get a sudden opportunity to skyrocket their professional career because of one call, made by a powerful connection, that mentors and champions such artists?

I'm a storytelling advocate. But I'm also known as a unifier and super-connector, with a "Rolodex" that I built over 30 years. I'm fortunate enough to have access to the best of the best worldwide, from agents, managers, celebrities, studio execs, distributors, international producers, and financiers. I was not an overnight success. I chose strategically and aligned myself with people I admired.

These people are my reputation protectors to this day.

I am often invited to listen to pitches, and I observe the content creators as they interact with me. There is a pattern when those pitch sessions go south- I have seen it as well while sharing the stage as a panelist at the Women in Entertainment Distribution Conference, for the Filming In Italy event, and the Hanè Saga Storytelling conference in Utah.

I was on a yacht in Cannes where my clients were pitched this little movie called "CODA." Indeed, it was not a typical Summit title after Hunger Games, Anna, or La La Land. But I can tell you one thing: all theatrical distributors who were output partners at Lionsgate wanted to be in business with Patrick Wachsberger.

Many balked at the "smallness" and not having major talent on board of "Coda". Still, Patrick's reputation for his winning instincts and the relationships he built over the years had the first round of buyers sign on to the film before production.

You can make these alliances, too, with three easy, actionable steps:

- **Invite a leader to lunch**
  You may not have the perfect logline, sales sheet pitch, deck, script, or sizzle but if you have a small budget to invest in sharing a meal with someone who can help your career, do that.

There is nothing like two people sitting at a table across from one another and conversing about life. Plus, you get the executive away from office distractions.

When he first started working in Hollywood, Brian Grazer was working as an assistant in a studio lot. He would go into an empty office and call all the people he ultimately wanted to work with on his lunch break. Grazer sometimes would call them for months until finally, they would accept. He was curious about people and their life stories and made some of the most important movies and shows of our time as a result of creating meaningful connections.

- **Be open to feedback**

I have seen writers, filmmakers, or even producers who do not accept critique from anybody way too many times.

The content creators who are the most humble and easy to work with are the ones that decision-makers prefer to hire. We will take nice and kind over perfect and arrogant.

Therefore, be open to the feedback of those who have been around longer than you. You are asked for adjustments to your material for good reasons. They're not trying to destroy your work. They're trying to make it better from a perspective of experience.

- **Ask questions**

Show interest and curiosity towards the person or company you want to do business with. It's not about their credits, or whether they work with the biggest stars in Hollywood or they made box office successes.

It's about finding particular things about their persona that drew your attention in the first place. You may have seen their animal advocacy work, or perhaps they are specific sports fans, or they profess that they had a unique mindset or approach behind their successful careers.

You will be amazed how shared commonalities and interests can become a solid relationship foundation.

The most powerful reputation-destroyers, destroyers.

Here is a truth nugget: the biggest turnoff and relationship destroyers I know are rooted in the ego and are easy to spot. Here are the most common ones.

YOU TALK ABOUT YOUR PROJECT NON-STOP

I have listened to pitches where there is no courtesy hello or small talk. You don't even know my name or what I have done in the Industry as far as I know. This is a huge turnoff, showing a lack of manners and pure selfishness.

YOU SEE THE PRODUCER AS A MEAL TICKET

You think that everything is due to you. The producer is not a bank, nor is sitting on a couch idle just waiting for a straightforward moneymaker that you believe you have to offer them. A producer is a champion who will be there by your side to help see your work get produced, sold, and distributed. They're not a stepping stone for you, to make you famous or rich, for you to discard once you get what you want.

Hollywood is no walk in the park, but you have to remember that a producer or an executive will be able to tell right away if you're looking at them as a way to benefit you and only you versus getting to know them and making sure that they will be your partner, your ally, your collaborator and treated with value and respect.

YOU DO NOT KNOW IT ALL

I have been in meetings or on calls with content creators to tell me that they know the business more than I do. When they have been around only a few months, they base their "know everything" on what they have read and not what they have experienced. The ones who have the experience never pretend to know everything. They always strive to learn from others and get different perspectives because the business is constantly in flux.

"If I take care of my character, my reputation will take care of itself."

- D.L. Moody

The creation of opportunity from professional experience through authentic connections will not only be financially rewarding in the long run. Still, it will open up pathways you never even knew existed and make the journey to success more enjoyable and lasting.

That I know for sure.

WHEN FOMO GETS IN THE WAY OF YOUR CREATIVE WORK

FOMO: (Fear of Missing Out) – that anxiety that an exciting or interesting event may currently be happening elsewhere, often aroused by posts seen on social media.

Have you ever found yourself scrolling your Instagram, Twitter, or Facebook for hours, lingering on those posts where mega deals are entered into by your fellow Artists? Or as they go LIVE on their Social to show off being on set on a film or TV show?

Are you feeling dejected when friends, your fellow artists, or even total strangers post about their fabulous lives and prolific careers?

With so much uncertainty surrounding us, it is as easy to get sucked into FOMO as it is into depression. Both seem interconnected.

While I have been a champion of community and information for Hollywood longevity, I am also acutely aware of how addictive social media can be and both its positive and negative psychological effects.

Artists and Content Creators are generally compassionate souls. We pour our hearts into those script pages, those acting roles, framing that perfect shot, pitching our passion project in the room. Rejection is constant. But when it is experienced directly, it is more easily handled, mainly if we are fueled by passion and determination. When it is experienced indirectly, I call it the "Why not Me Syndrome," it can create a sleuth of self-doubt, the most dangerous and stagnant emotion of all, in my opinion.

During the Pandemic, I also experienced FOMO in spades. While looking for those signs of the needle moving in the Entertainment Industry, I got lost in the happy and exciting personal lives of others, with a mixture of celebration but also a hint of dejection and, let me be honest, even envy.

I have always been very confident in my work due to being 30 years in the Business (hello, I am still here!) and being a fierce advocate for constant learning and authentic networking.

But for me, marriages, baby births, travel photos, extended family gatherings, and vast and new business successes outside of my world, after seeing our Entertainment Industry crumble for the past few years, have been tough to digest. Possibly because when our FIRE is put out (if we are obsessed creators like yours truly), then we notice the things we should have given more time to and did not, such as personal and everyday life, and that emptiness becomes palpable.

To fight this FOMO or more like embracing it, I poured my energy into leveling up my spiritual growth and Mindset. I talk about this on my Season 3 Episode 1 podcast.

So, I am going to give you some practical and Mindset tips to help your FOMO be gone. It worked wonders for me, and it was all done by trial and error.

The Practical FOMO Cure.

Go on a digital detox.

Put your phone down or turn it to airplane mode. Silence all notifications on your computer. Don't read about those mega-deals in the Trades. Put that news in a separate folder and read it only once a week.

Turn off the News.

Believe me, if a natural disaster is looming, the news will get to you somehow. The Pandemic brainwashing is creating long-term PTSD in all of us.

Stop doing too many of too many things.

You do not need to write 10 movies, binge-watch, or send hundreds of emails like a robot. Practice the Pomodoro Technique (See Chapter 5).

There is something of great value in intentionality and essentialism. Do a Marie Kondo on your entire life.

Stop posting just to get a one-up on others on your extraordinary life.

The more authentic you are, the better relationships you will attract.

The Mindset FOMO hacks.

1. Dig deep to find out what you truly want - an actual want is not a wish but an outcome.

2. What outcomes in all areas of your life and your projects do you want to happen? List them in practical and attainable baby steps.

3. Meditate on how you feel when they happen.

We are in the Business of MOVING IMAGES, so it should be easier for you to do. The more vivid and detailed the image of the outcome, the stronger the feeling.

Share your emotions and put them on paper.

Reread those when tempted to get hypnotized by your Facebook, Twitter, or IG feed.

"Money is the byproduct of doing the right thing. "

This is one of the personally created mantras that has reminded me of all that happens at the right time and with the right state of mind.

I look forward to your feedback as you move out of FOMO, Fear of Missing Out, and head into MASH, Making Authentic Shit Happen.

7 LIFE HACKS FOR CREATIVES

When you are going after your creative dreams, the years seem to go by fast, especially if the results of the hard work do not become palpable. It's never too late to take stock of what has been accomplished and amplify all the right actions or course adjustments to finish the year with a bang.

I believe in growth on both a personal and professional level. Next-level greatness is only accessible if we know how to do a regular check-in ourselves and take inventory of where and how our energy is spent. As Aristotle has said: "We are what we repeatedly do. Excellence is not an act but a habit."

A longevity of 30 years brings gifts. I have applied myself on many levels, from branding to marketing, to selling to learning how to finance, network, create marketing materials, and be authentic and truthful to my brand, mission, and why.

If you are feeling stagnant in your career, I am sharing my toolbox of wisdom to help you level up.

I did not invent the wheel. My knowledge has been attained through self-development, investing, and learning from the pros. There is power in surrounding yourself with those who have succeeded in their field. I have sat in rooms where Oscar-winning films were greenlit, and projects came to life only to become Box Office record-breakers.

I ended up applying the life hacks below more during the pandemic. They enabled me to be more fulfilled in every area of my life.

1. Thank You notes.

I know that sounds old school, but thank you notes are some of the most valuable and long-term relationship-building tools you could ever use for yourself. I had on one of my podcasts this season mega-producer Vin Di Bona, from America's Funniest Videos and Entertainment Tonight, and his beautiful wife, Erica Gerard De Bona. We met at the Italian Television Festival, where I am a member of the Advisory Board. Destiny brought me to sit down with them.

I learned that Erica Girard wrote a book about the power of thank-you notes. She was a production executive and has used thank-you notes to build those long-lasting relationships. Back in the day, when we were selling movies, I used that hack, and it delivered- big time. I was to get a film to sell. Back in the day, not many movies were produced, certainly not as many as they are today, and people were competing to get the rights to sell those movies. I sent the Producer a fax- I just wanted to acknowledge the lady representing the movie and thank her for coming in. I wished her all success from the bottom of my heart, even if it wasn't something that would eventually be represented and sold by us.

Because we approached the project with humanity, kindness, integrity, authenticity, and the thank you note, we ended up having a movie that everybody was bidding for.

Oprah said, during Super Soul Sunday:
One of the things that people need the most is to feel seen and understood.

That goes a long way, much more than any sales gimmick.

2.   Gratitude.

Do a 100-day gratitude challenge, where for 100 days straight, you will write three things you are grateful for. Gratitude is a form of prayer. And when you are thankful, you're acknowledging God, the universe, the higher power for the bountiful and the blessings that you get to have. And if you learn to appreciate the little things, the big things will also come to you.

3.   Pitch like a pro.

I have been selling other people's projects and brands all my life. In 2021 I took some classes on how to have a concrete framework for successful pitching based on a combination of mindset and business tricks. I put together the perfect pitch masterclass with my proprietary technique that I ended up teaching at the Thessaloniki

Animation Film Festival. Authentic non-robotic pitching will be needed more, as in today's world, people have ADD. There's so much information out there, so many people doing the selling, some of it a bit slimy, if you ask me, with buzzwords and false representations.

I believe that your pitch will pop when you get clear on your why, which is why you do what you do. Who are you? What do you represent? What are your values, and how do you want them to translate into your storytelling? Then your pitching will be so much clearer and will have more impact. But it does take skills. It does take practice.

4. Branding.

Another is from this year's favorite book, "Hook Point" by Brendan Kane. Brendan Kane is somebody who did the branding and the imaging for Taylor Swift and a lot of celebrities. It applies to anybody, a filmmaker trying to sell a project in a room, a producer, a financier. How to stand out in a 30-second world is gold.

5. IRL.

It stands for IN REAL LIFE. I know everybody's talking about Metaverse and the virtual world, which I think will be the future. But nothing beats actual human connections. I do not mean Zoom. Let's just get out of the house if we can, get a drink together, and look at each other in the eyes. There's nothing like the electricity and the energy exchanged between people getting to know one another, body language. The most prominent relationships I've nurtured and shepherded for decades always brought a result somewhere in my life. Sometimes you do not know it.

Sometimes you meet someone, and you think they're going to be financing a movie, but then they end up becoming your best friend. Sometimes you meet someone that starts as a friendship, and then they end up helping you sell your project or introduce you to somebody who will give you leverage for your film. So, make a point to reach out to people and ask them out.

6. Digital Detox.

It is vital. You need to just nurture our souls and hearts by being in silence and not talking about business. Stop scrolling over Instagram and Facebook and look at what everybody is doing. If you just listen to your voice and take some time off to ask yourself, what do I want? What do I want? And keep asking that question? What do I want? Because sometimes the first, What do I want? Will get you the surface answers. Who do you want to be? What would you like to have more of?

If you can do it for a whole week, your life will change. I promise you.

7. Go beyond your comfort zone.

During the last year, I have taken more courses and more educational things on things that have nothing to do with show business. I learned about YouTube, how to be in the quantum field, and much more. I just kept reading more books about screenwriting and producing, and I listened to people speak on the virtual stage. Because nobody is truly a pro at something by staying stagnant. You always have to keep leveling up.

THINK LIKE AN AD MAN [USING CREATIVE AGENCY TECHNIQUES TO BUILD IDENTITY]

One of my favorite TV series is Mad Men. When Don Draper walks into a room with his ideas and visual pitches for a potential client, he does it impeccably, and with as few images and slogans as possible to sell the product.

His theory has proof in the pudding: *"You are the product. You are feeling something, that's what sells."*

This is precisely why we all are glued to our television screens during the Super Bowl to watch the commercials that make us tear up or incite some other emotion within us. When it happens, we talk about it on social media. Whether or not we realize it or not, those digital conversations contribute to the brand's reach.

So how does this approach apply to your creative work? You're not trying to sell an ad.

Maybe you're not, but I'm here to tell you that you are always selling something. It could be someone who reads your material and believes they can take it to the next level. Or it could be an actor who wants to star in your film, a financier with a big fat checkbook, a fan who will rave about your film (thus increasing its revenue), or a festival that will accept and showcase your work.

I am asking you, while you read this blog, to think like Don Draper.

I have seen hundreds of "leave-behind materials" for finished films, films in development, films in production, scripts for sale, books for adaptation, reality series, and mini-series. You name it, I have seen it. I have also read short packages, and long packages, perused websites, watched sizzles, and even more mood trailers.

For me, these materials got me to say YES or NO in my head before I read the script or watched the movie. This is because I had an emotional reaction and wanted to have an immersive experience within the world I was watching or reading about.

Below are some thoughts to help you trigger your introspection, followed by short tips for applying the "ad man mentality" to improve your presentations, visual or written, as well as your overall brand.

Why Should I Care?

This is something your audience will ask themselves the moment they turn the page or click the play button. The scenes have to suck them into your world, written or shot, and make them feel.

If I am a horror fan, I need a good kill.
If I am an adrenaline junkie, I want to believe I am also in danger.
If I am a hopeless romantic, push my dream girl (or boy) button and woo me to fall in love with your protagonist.

Don't Tell Me How to Feel. Show Me.

The opening scene is everything, so make it a great one. Not because you want to convince me it is so, but because you truly want me to care. The first images of a trailer or sizzle have to give me a high.

Anything slow to build, dialogue-heavy, or has poor quality production is not going to do it.

Do you watch local commercials? Most likely not, because many are amateur and don't evoke emotion. But you probably watch Super Bowl commercials. They are big and engaging and include elements that make us want to spend big money, and all because they evoke genuine feelings within you.

Don't Compare.

You are not here to persuade me to like you by comparing me to other equally likable things, projects, or movies that made it to the big screen. That's just as bad as taking someone out on a date and convincing them to keep dating you by talking about other men or women you dated. I would not feel flattered, would you? Nobody wants a copycat. Don't believe the Hollywood hype.

In a world of remakes and reboots where we think originality has failed, there has always been a fresh take on an original idea that made the unoriginal become original. As an executive, I do not need to see pie charts with box office numbers of similar movies. If I can't guess it on my own, then your project was not clear enough. If this is the case, you should reconsider all the points made in the paragraphs above.

Therefore, as you prepare your pitch deck, your business plan, your sizzle, your trailer, your marketing package, your Facebook page, and your website, remember another Don Draper piece of advice: **If you don't like what is being said, change the conversation.**

If your buyer or your audience doesn't get goosebumps from your creative genius, please remember the following ad man tricks and essentials for your project's identity:

Be Visual: Communicate through images.

Be Meaningful: Ask friends and associates if the essence of your brand cultivates an emotion (hopefully not disgust), and how strong that emotion is. Take a survey and re-calibrate accordingly.

Don't Blend in, Stand Out: You need to make yourself and your work memorable. Use simple names and buzzwords that bring about a feeling of uniqueness and novelty. Don't think like an author, think like an ad man. Your slogan tells the story.

Think Ahead: Make your work timeless. Make it something that can become a cult in the future or conversation-worthy for the years to come. One of the biggest mistakes I see in packages is the mentioning of franchises, installments, or thinking years ahead for your series. If your work is timeless, I will be the one who will want to franchise or merchandise it or spin it off. I won't need your pitch for it.

Open Your World to the Audience: Accessibility is everything. Any movie, book, comic book, or series that stood the test of time was not obscure or hard to understand. It managed to draw attention, even from its not-obvious audience. If people can easily interpret it, they will google it for years to come.

I wish you all to draw out of your work the best "wow factor you can find!

Happy Marketing!

HOW A TOMATO CAN HELP YOU MEET YOUR WRITING & FILMMAKING DEADLINES

I am an obsessive multi-tasker.
Some call me a master juggler.

I can work on any given day on multiple projects and activities. I'm not sure if it is because I love variety or because deep down, I am a masochist. Or a control freak.

From buying films on behalf of our theatrical distributor clients, selling and marketing those films, developing content for film and television, and representing personalities, influencers, or media companies, I do it all. I also consult Wall Street and do story development consultations.

My phone should be surgically attached to my body, as I receive and write an average of 500 emails a day. While I do all of these things, I kid myself that I can also find the time to go to the gym, follow my social media, and have a semblance of a personal life. At times I get so involved in what I am doing (including writing and pitching) that I forget to eat.

Or, to another extreme, I completely forget my boundaries and let meaningless phone calls, emails, or meetings take me to the land of nowhere and off-focus. Bottom line, I sometimes think I'm Super Woman. But at what expense? My master juggling superpower can leave me drained and unable to say NO or to prioritize because I want to be able to do it all and do it great.

I end up getting lost in activities that aren't really at the top of my priority list and when I have to meet a deadline, I am so stressed by the passing of time that I start forgetting what the first thing was I started this morning. My to-do list scribbles become more and more disjointed, and everything becomes a matter of life and death.

But is **EVERYTHING** truly that important?

There has to be a way to control this do people like you and me who write, produce, create, direct, and sell, or suffer from plain old **ADD**? And there is.

The Discovery of the Tomato

After the Cannes Film Festival, I went to Italy to visit my family. While on the freeway I stopped by a gas station that also had a store with various items, including books. My lucky stars must have shined on me that day as my eye caught the title of a book by Italian author Francesco Cirillo, called The Pomodoro Technique (Pomodoro is tomato in Italian.)

It appears this is a very famous method for time management for the individual and an entire team. The image was that of a kitchen timer shaped like a Tomato. I just had to buy it. In a very fast and easy read, I could not believe how simple the solution was to a calmer, more effective way to work with focus and to complete actions by order of importance. Upon my return to the US, I decided to test this technique, and it does work. Even now, as I write this Stage 32 blog, I am using the Pomodoro Technique. I am three tomatoes in at this point of my writing and should be finished with another two tomatoes.

How many times have you been drowning in your work, with little time, distractions, interruptions, and delays?

The objective of the Pomodoro Technique is to increase concentration, and awareness of decisions, and give the right estimate of completion of any given task. This is done through a different way of looking at time.

Here are the only three things you need:

Kitchen Timer *(It doesn't have to be shaped like a tomato, although I bought a cute one for myself in the shape of a black cat as I love cats!)*

Some paper

A journal

The paper is for a TO DO list and should include the date, a list of things to be done within the day in order of priority, and a separate column that should be titled: Unexpected and Urgent.

The journal is to log activities that are made of your to-dos and shouldn't be marked completed at the end of the day.

Next to it will also be the number of tomatoes it took to accomplish that activity.

The tomato itself represents a fraction of the time of 25 minutes. That is what you set your timer for. For each tomato time fraction concluded, there needs to be a 5-minute break (water, bathroom, check your email, write new tasks and reminders that came to mind), but they need to be done within 5 minutes. These 25-minute segments are used only for ONE TASK, whatever that task may be. You cannot break from that and start something else.

No distractions are allowed, and you need to exercise some discipline.

How to Use Tomatoes in Scriptwriting

If you want to write a script, those 25 minutes are for scriptwriting only. When you are on the 5-minute break, if you check your email or Facebook, it is not recommended you respond (not even a like or love button push), as it can take you away from the task. If an email or voicemail comes in during the 25-minute activity segment, you will have to hold on responding and send all your messages to voicemail. So basically, if there is an action to be done, it can wait till you are done with your goal. (For example, writing 5 pages of a script).

Make sure you write these new to-do things (that may have transpired during breaks and have nothing to do with writing) in your journal in order of priority. Then forget about them for a while. Every 4 tomatoes (or every 2 hours) your break becomes longer. Eventually, it will be 15 to 30 minutes. This is the perfect time to make coffee, take a walk, do breathing exercises, play with your pet, or respond to simple emails and messages. Do not do anything too involved.

If you finish the task before the tomato (timer) starts ringing, you can use the rest of the time to reflect on what you just did and acknowledge it in the activity at hand. Or go back and review your writing, for

example. Once you're done with the entire task, you'll know how many tomatoes it took you so next time you can estimate your time better.

Segmenting time in this way can be incredibly therapeutic for many reasons.

To begin with, you do not panic if you have to write an entire screenplay or presentation because every 5, 10, or 15 pages you write, you'll be able to celebrate your victories. This, of course, applies to even personal activities like cleaning, working out, or meditating. When it's time to make calls, do them all at the same time, in a focused way.

The tomato also allows you to get good at boundary setting. Say a friend text you to go to dinner that night. Is that a life-or-death situation? Can it not wait till you at least get through four tomatoes? It will be helpful also as you log in your tomatoes to put small x marks on how many times you were interrupted by others because it will indicate how you manage your boundaries as you get good at this.

Here are some helpful tips for you:

- If you are unable to finish the tomato and fall victim to distraction (by your own doing or an outside source), do not get mad at yourself. Just start a new tomato.

- If you're working with others, let them also do the Pomodoro Technique with you. This way you can all meet up at break, and everyone puts in the same effort on any given project.

- Use a kitchen timer. There are apps on the App Store that you can download, if you search for the Pomodoro Technique. They are pretty great but until you master it, the loud sound of the kitchen timer is an excellent way for your brain to understand the start and stop process.

- Protect your tomato at all costs. If someone interrupts you, the best course of action is to inform them of your unavailability and briefly negotiate to postpone the interruption. You can return the call or answer that email after one, two, or three tomatoes, depending on the urgency.

These are the basic principles. As I write this last paragraph, I am thrilled to say I finished within schedule. I can't wait to hear feedback on this and on how this technique worked for you.

My confidence in being able to work on something distraction-free has skyrocketed as has my boundary-setting ability. Saying no has just become easier for me and all this is because of a tomato!

Now a *real* Italian tomato is something else and is best used to make great sauce for pasta, which you can cook for yourself to celebrate your new time management skills.

One Tomato, Two Tomatoes, Three Tomatoes.

Start Counting!

HOW BODY LANGUAGE & BUZZWORDS CAN DRASTICALLY IMPROVE YOUR PITCH

You got yourself a face-to-face meeting with a decision-maker. This is epic, could be a game-changer, you think. This is your "one shot, one opportunity to seize everything you ever wanted in one moment" says the Eminem song, your anthem playing on rotation on your Spotify as you sit in the Lobby of the office of the producer you most want to meet who would make your script or book into a movie, or the sales agent or distributor that finance your project, or that Top 5 Agent that could put you, yes you, in his or her exclusive client roster, amongst the best of the best.

You finally get in the room, you sit on the couch and you start firing off your log line and your pitch. You have been rehearsing for days. You know you got this. And after your delivery, crickets. Or a request to see your script said in a lackluster tone. Or maybe a rushed handshake, thanking you for coming and you will be hearing from them soon. Which you know is a lie, as after that no follow-up email from your side gets replied to, or you just get a "sorry, this is not for us, best of luck to you" generic pass. What just happened here?

Do you ever listen to your gut? Because if you did, you would know how you did, and you would feel elated, knowing you just made an ally in the Industry, no matter what. Here enter the two magic skills that when studied and practiced will help you make a lasting impression in the room. Those skills don't need a psychology degree, just some good observation skills and the power of being present. There are books you can read, but I am here to give you some clear signs you can recognize in another and body language you can give to help you in the face-to-face interaction of a decision-maker.

THE YAWN - your executive starts yawning. Then he justifies it with lack of sleep, working long hours, stressful days, and not being properly caffeinated. The truth is – you are boring! I can assure you; a yawn is easy to suppress if they are intoxicated by your charming personality.

THE FIDGET - your executive keeps moving his body around, crossing his legs, uncrossing his legs, playing with a pen, or a stress ball, or his arms are just locked into a tight self-embrace. What this means is he or she can't wait for this to be over. They are wondering when you are going to just shut up, or how many more meetings have to go by before they show you the door.

THE DEAD EYE - The executive just won't look at you. Or staring at you as if you were a ghost. What crosses the executive's mind is how they are going to fake interest once the meeting is over, or they are just thinking about lunch, drinks, dinners, or who else they are going to see after you.

THE MULTI-TASKER - The executive is writing emails while you speak. He is texting, playing with his or her phone, and they are swiping right on Tinder. Of course, their excuse is they are on a deadline, or there is a crisis happening. What this means is they can't wait for you to get out of there so they can do something more enjoyable than listening to you

And lastly-
THE LACK OF INTERVENTION - The executive asks no questions. He or she is not curious about what happens next. They don't ask you what you are working on beyond this pitch, or anything about you and what drives you. Your Buzz words do not have him or her buzzing.

Don't be depressed. Here comes the good stuff, because you can use body language yourself and buzz words to shine in the room. I am going to outline the basic ones that you need to feel like a million bucks.

EYE CONTACT - If you need to imagine your executive naked to get over stage fright, go ahead. Because you are going to look in their eyes. A lot. Pretend for a minute you are a rockstar, and you are sitting in front of your fans. You are so grateful they are there to hear you out, you want them to know you see them, that your pitch/your song, is especially for them.

USE OBSERVATION FOR CONVERSATION - Look around the room, do you see pictures of spouses, dogs, kids, Oscars, their favorite Sports Team? This is the perfect opportunity to comment. Find some common ground. Example: " I see you are a Rams fan, can you believe they are in the Super Bowl?". This is establishing a connection that makes the interaction more personable. You acknowledge they are human beings, like you.

THROW A POP QUIZ - During your pitch, ask them a question relating to your plot twist, your character arc, and your genre to make sure they are listening. Ask them if they have any questions for you. If they do not remember what you said a minute ago, chances are you need to refocus their attention on you. Hence, throw yourself a lifeline with the next tip…

WHAT IS THEIR DREAM PROJECT? - Ask them flat out, what movie they wish they could have made and did not. Or what is the TV show they must binge? Everyone has a DREAM project- focus on the buzzword and see their eyes sparkle. Now you know if your pitch is even in their emotional sphere and if not, time to jump overboard and improvise with another idea or script that you are working on.

MAKE THEM RELATE TO YOU - As you pitch, personalize your story by giving a few keywords about how you got to write, produce, and direct this story. Use "LOVE' and "LIKE" and "ADMIRE" frequently. Or why you are passionate about this. Do not tell them what they should think about your pitch. Let them decide if it is the next blockbuster Oscar winner or Hit Show. Don't be afraid to give some information about your past or your interest beyond the pitch. Keep it short. Keep it sweet.

And here comes the most important piece of advice I can give you.

Tell them **WHY** you are there, not because they are going to finance your film, or buy your script, or they were one of the thousand calls or emails you made. Make them feel special. Remind them about the films they made, and how you enjoyed going to see them. Congratulate them on an Oscar win, a box office outcome. Or if you know anything about the executive's background, their struggles to get to the top, their special skills, or a quote they gave in an interview that stayed with you, let them know that.

I for one, become always open and receptive to **REAL CONNECTION** with those that approach me. I practice all the above when needing someone to help me or my clients go the extra mile. I rarely have seen it fail me.

Do not be attached to the outcome. Even if they don't ask to read your script or see your movie, chances are they will feel good about having given you their time, and your gut will thank you. You will be confident, motivated, and ready to receive the YES you have been waiting for so long to hear.

DESPISE THE FREE LUNCH – HOW TO GET PAID LIKE A PRO

Getting paid for being a filmmaker is an art form and rarely taken to heart, so artists starve for their craft. This image of the "starving artist" must not and should not be perpetuated. Most people believe that the work of a writer, a producer, or a filmmaker is based on passion alone, and as a result, it is assumed that all artists are meant to work for free, or to get paid later, because of their passion for the craft will make them accept work under any condition, including the freebies or the infamous "defer".

Of course, the compensation for your talent and skill should be directly proportional to your experience, but I have seen it one time too many when a seasoned and experienced writer filmmaker producer, or actor is asked to join a project with promises of riches that are broken one time too many, leaving the artist spirit shattered and bank account depleted.

I am here to give you some advice on how to start giving yourself more value and how to value your peers as well: you get paid if they need your art and your talent and you pay them as well if you need theirs. Becoming more resolute in this will make you feel empowered and will also avoid too many misunderstandings or backstabbers within your Team as you embark on putting together or selling your next movie or show.

One of my favorite books for navigating the shark-infested waters of Hollywood is "The 48 Laws of Power" By Robert Greene. Law 40 is called: "Despise the Free Lunch". It clearly says (and gives true historical facts to prove its point) that what is offered for free is dangerous- it usually involves either a trick or a hidden obligation.

WHAT IS WORTH IS WORTH PAYING FOR.

By paying your way you stay clear of gratitude, guilt, and deceit. It is also wise to pay the full price- there are no cutting corners with excellence.

I can hear the stir of protest here, as pretty much everyone I know, even well-known directors, producers, and writers, are looking for money, not chomping at the bits to give it away.

However, let me offer you some solutions here in the main categories of writing, directing, and producing, a compromise of sorts, so you can look at yourself in the mirror and not feel like an art whore, because sorry to be so blunt, but even whores do not give it away for free. And how you position yourself (which is directly reflected by your resume), can make a world of a difference in negotiating for yourself a fair compensation, or at least a fair barter between you and your cohorts.

Scenario 1-

You are a writer, and a producer or director asks you to do a rewrite of a script of yours or another's IP and they ask you to do it for free. Here are some questions to ask yourself before even attempting to negotiate a rate for yourself. Is the director or producer in question an A-lister? If so, then you will get something of value in return for rewriting for little or no money as most likely that project will get made sooner or later and you can also add this collaboration to your resume.

Consider it an investment in your career by asking that your name be mentioned in a press release and that you are allowed to participate in a creative process. The second question to ask yourself: is there any cash funding in place? If so, there is no excuse that a gesture of payment cannot be made to you. You are a Team player, you won't ask for the moon and stars, but if a project has actual funding and a producer or director cannot spare a few thousand dollars to send your way, there is something wrong with this picture.

On the reverse, if you are a newbie writer, and you want a filmmaker or producer to join your Team and take your project to the next level, meaning you need them more than they need you, you have to show you are willing to pay them for their expertise, in whatever way you can afford. Believe me, the money wasted in screenwriting competitions (if you add them up) or in pitching interns at various pitch festivals, is far greater than partnering up with the real Pros who will open doors for you- assuming that a Producer or Director in question has the credits and experience to make it worth your while.

Scenario 2-

You are a director, and you are asked to be attached to a script or project. If there is no funding in place, and you like the Team, you should negotiate for yourself a down payment upon first development funds being secured. If the Writer or Producer asks for you to do a sizzle reel, visual trailer, or prepare a storyboard to sell the project, unless the Writer or Producer is going to enhance your image (see Scenario 1 above) because they are fairly high profile and have a specific game plan to make things happen, you must ask for some compensation for any additional work required of you such as putting together mood trailers. Everybody who wants to make a career in any area has a credit card they can tap into to pay with a symbolic amount of acknowledgment for their talent and visual skills.

On the reverse, if you need a bona fide (emphasis on bona fide) producer to shepherd your project, take it to film markets or help you put together a viable business plan, or a line producer to do a budget for you that will help your funding or a casting director to give you access to talent, please find a way to pay them something. Here again, you can take advantage of credit cards if short on cash.

Scenario 3-

You are a producer who has access to international co-production partners, or distribution, or can run a set seamlessly and you have the credits to prove it and you are asked to attach to a project. It is perfectly okay to ask for a percentage of your producer fee upfront because legendary producer Dino De Laurentis once said to me "NO producer, NO movie" You are the only key that opens the doors, so ask for the money that reflects the blood sweat and tears of your experience level.

On the other hand, you are a producer who needs to attach a director or needs a certain type of writer who will increase the value of your passion project. Pay them! An established director, with a deposit against his or her fee, will go the extra mile to give visibility to your film and will attract actors. A showrunner writer from a hit TV show or a writer who has box office hits in his resume, will make your material shine and allow you entry to the key broadcasters and Studio producers. And if you need a quick polish from a writer, give them something.

The bottom line, asking to get paid for being an "artist" is not an act of greed but of necessity to keep the checks and balances in proper order. There will be more times that you get screwed in a movie or television show than not, therefore whatever money you will have gotten to date will come in very handy to pay a therapist.

I have gone over the 3 main categories but this, of course, applies to actors, cinematographers, editors, composers, casting directors, line producers, etc.

Don't let anyone push the buttons of your passion for your craft as an excuse to work for free. Carefully choose your associates and teammates. If they can't value you at the get-go, chances are they will feel the same after you defer your fees or work on commission. Being liked, like a love affair, is a fragile and temporary state.

Do you want to be respected for your talents? Show them your price tag!

HOW TO FIND THE HIGHWAY OUT OF DEVELOPMENT HELL

In our ever-so-wonderful and creative La La Land, there is a crowded little neighborhood called Development Hell. The real estate that sits there can potentially be worth millions, but the building phase is excruciatingly long. So long, that the developers and architects behind it often give up altogether or turn it over and sell it back for scraps. This is the sad place where creativity and passion are replaced by stagnancy and frustration.

If you've ever optioned a project, that great novel or screenplay or television show, and felt you were "off to the races" because a producer or even yourself, believed you were now easily going to speed through the necessary steps that would lead you and your team into production, only to find yourself months or years later with no sign of progress and your dreams still just a piece of paper, rest assured you are not alone. You probably see yourself there now, roaming around aimlessly in what appears a creative ghost town as you have yet to meet a money man, a bankable actor, a visionary director, a studio, a distributor, or a partner, who could lead you out of your misery and show you the Highway out of this hell hole.

Stuck in a loop, you start reading news about other movies moving ahead. But not yours.
Other shows are being greenlit.
But not yours.
You feel helpless. You do not want to give up, and you begin to question your sanity.
Why them and not me?

Because I have been there myself, and I have seen many projects crash and burn, including my own and those of my clients, I am here to show you a way forward and a way out. I do not promise an arrival to the destination, but I know there are things you can do to lead you toward a path that can get you to the Highway where you can leave this Hell Hole (pardon the pun) and feel like you still have a shot.

Before I get to pointing out the rainbow of hope, let me tell you some obvious reasons why you and your project are in Development Hell:

- You got so excited about bragging about the accomplishment of being an "optioned" writer to all your friends and family, even if that option paid you a handful of dollars or just $1, that you forgot to research the person or company that secured your IP. Is your producer experienced? Or is this a company or person that has never made a film or show like yours, or has the connections to get you there but is hoping to make it big on your dime?

- Does he or she regularly update you on their activities for your IP? Have you given them a one or two-year option that binds you to the producer or company, regardless of performance?

- Your producer, partner, or production company brags they have access to funding and have secured the funding for your project because your IP is so awesome, and investors just read your script or projects and were wowed. They even show you Proof of Funds (POF), but somehow this document does not spell out the name of your project or script or the terms in which the funds will be released to get you into production. Months go by, and all you do is hang out with that document and those mystery investors that you never met or spoke to while zero money is being released to even get you to the stage to start casting or securing distribution, both being the two most important things that give investors a comfort level for the dollars they allegedly are releasing for your wonderful script or project.

- Your producer or production company has you undertake dozens of rewrites, letting you believe that your material is not ready until they say so. You, out of your eagerness to please, accept any notes (though interestingly enough those notes do not come from the feedback of an attached director, interested cast member, or real financier) only to find your IP having many voices and directions while losing your own.

- Your producer or production company is unable to "go with the flow," meaning they remain stuck to a certain required budget, cast, or director they feel will bring about the green light or finance of your IP. As we all know, Hollywood is a fast-moving

Highway and a business model that, after six months, can often become obsolete and require course adjustment. But stubbornness prevails, and here you are in Development Hell town drinking yourself into oblivion as the very team that is supposed to facilitate your goals and dreams hinders them.

- You, your producer, or financier (if you have found by now one that is writing the checks) have unrealistic expectations of packaging. You go after actors who are busy for the next couple of years, but you are convinced that if you have the money and they read you, they will jump ship from any other project they are on to join yours. And the agents and managers will applaud the process. Or you go after actors and directors that are out of your financial budget range for the same reason, forgetting the majority of the time, it's all about the money, otherwise, you would not see great actors in shitty movies. That's because they got a HUGE payday!

- You get where I am going with this, I hope. This brings me to one easy ticket to get you off the Highway of Development Hell and merry-go-round that makes you want to puke. JUST SAY NO! You have given yourself six months or even a year. Let me tell you the real truth here: If there is not any forward movement something is wrong, most of the time is due to one or all of the above 5 points.

Therefore, here are some tips, and some fuel to your fire:

- Hire a lawyer or get the advice of a lawyer to get you out of the Option Agreement. Or, if you have not signed one, do yourself a favor and have contingencies on your option that have to do with progress and performance. We all know it can take years to make a film or sell a TV show and you want to know that at least your partners are doing the work and trying their best and have the connections to keep your IP alive.

- If you are told there are "investors," ask to speak to them. Find out why they are allegedly putting money into your project and what they are expecting in return. If they exist. Remember "Jerry McGuire?" You may want to start using the saying "Show me the Money" more often, especially when it comes to investors. Or, at the very least, find out their net worth or track record of investing is a legitimate one.

- If you are asked to do more than five rewrites, stop. Put that in your agreement and make sure you are clear as you hand over your IP that any other rewrites will be done only if truly necessary and by the notes of soon-to-be-attached actors and directors or viable feedback of actual and future distributors and financiers.

- If you see that after six months nothing has happened with your script or project, not even a hopeful possibility, change the course. Lower the budget. Turn the IP into a series. Increase your budget. Set the story elsewhere. Change the age of your characters or their race or gender. Whatever breathes new life into your IP.

- Movies or shows find their way to the big or small screen because of the teamwork of passionate creatives. Forget about reaching for that A-list actor. Find someone who has value and wants to do your film or show and tell everyone about it, including cutting his rates or telling his reps to help you. Or discover that visionary director who has that magnetic power and the crazy skills to wow anyone with his storyboards, mood reel, and storytelling angle. If he or she has the "it "factor and understands the material, they will sell it in the room. They will knock on every door to make sure the movie or show gets made. Most movies that we never forget were from filmmakers who told the story in a way that was never seen before. Spielberg, Eastwood, Gibson, Tarantino, the Scott Brothers, Bigelow. They are masters for a reason. They don't just make movies, they create memories.

Are you now ready to ride out of this Development Hell town?
Just like Dorothy, all you have to do is click your shoes and make a wish to be taken back on track, where you belong, and where your dreams still have a chance.

4 WAYS TO FAIL AS A PRODUCER (AND 4 WAYS TO SUCCEED!)

"Power is a place as well as a verb. It is inside the information tent." – Lynda Obst

The quote above is from Hello, He Lied, a must-read book on producing. The book is written by a trailblazer who did it all and saw it all, Lynda Obst. Being a female producer in Hollywood isn't easy. When I decided to expand my horizons and became a film producer, I felt I was ahead of the game because I knew what it took to finance a movie as a worldwide sales agent and distributor's rep.

How hard could it be to find a good script and turn it into a movie?

After all, it is said content is king, and there should be tons of avenues to get content onto the big screen. The avenues do exist, but as I started producing films, shorts, and documentaries, and learning by trial and error, I realized there is much more to the producer title.

You see, most people assume that a producer does only two things:
Options of the material.
Gets the money.

Nothing could be further from the truth.

This is the reason why Starbucks and The Coffee Bean are full of aspiring producers who end up doing the same things writers do: They pitch a project, expect another producer to be ready to provide funding for their project, and let someone else do all the work.

Let me be clear about something here as I hope to debunk the myths behind a producer: Most real producers are not rich, nor do they have or want to spend every cent to finance the next script that comes their way. Especially yours. Real producers know how to develop, make, and release movies - from the first moment they have their eye on a powerful story to the moment the film is distributed, including the huge effort and investment of all sorts of resources that comes with it.

Ironically, we the producers who produce from beginning to end are constantly solicited to purchase scripts for crazy money, as if we have millions sitting in a bank waiting to be spent. Content creators function under the assumption that we also have plenty of free time and are not good enough for a project to shepherd.

We are also frequently asked by writers to join projects (often without compensation) with the sole expectation that our job is of a fundraising nature, and only if we are worthy of the task do we deserve to get paid. It's as if our life was nothing until this script or that project came along, so we ought to drop everything we are doing to get working on it.

I am hoping with this post to give readers a newfound appreciation and respect for the job of a producer, as well as acknowledge my producing peers. When you call yourself a producer, you must understand what it entails, the surefire ways to fall on your face, and the very practical ways to become good at your job and earn the money that comes with the title.

You Will Fail If:

You Are Unable to Recognize the Market Value of Your Project.

A good producer has the ability and instinct to choose the material he or she wants to see made not only based on personal taste, but also based on proper evaluation to determine the inherent value of the intellectual property in the marketplace, and the audience it will or will not draw. As mentioned before, while content is king, the court (aka the audience) hails the king. If your film has a limited audience or market, you should be able to ascertain the effort involved and recognize if your project is current or will be current shortly. Be vigilant not to choose the wrong genre, the wrong audience, the wrong storyline, or the wrong medium.

You Are Unfamiliar with Film Financing Structure.

Development is everything. A good producer has done extensive research on the packaging of a script (with the above point in mind) by having an idea of the type of cast and director it wants to attract. But that's only a small part, and an uncertain one, to secure early on unless the producer has solid and long-standing relationships with actors and directors and their representatives.

If you think your script can stand on its legs and is enough to get financing, you are very likely to fail. You need to be well-versed in putting together realistic and accurate business plans that take into consideration all the ways a film can get funded. If you do not know about tax credits, co-production structures, how to secure distribution early on for your project, how to recognize potential financing sources (private and traditional ones), or how to present the project in a way that makes it attractive to interested financial and creative partners, you've got a lot of homework left to do.

You Are Irresponsible with The Investors' Money.

It is not enough to get the money. A good producer is responsible for every dollar he or she receives toward a project. Once they get their funding, they put most of it on the screen and not in their pockets. A good producer is smart enough to hire a line producer who will make the film look ten times its cost, even if it was made at a fraction of the cost.

A good producer will also try to leave some of the investment outside of physical production to invest in a great marketing and distribution campaign. Nothing is a sure thing, but it is important to prove to your investors that you did your best in every aspect from production to the film's release.

You Are Stubborn, and Not a Team Player.

Making movies is a team effort and everyone deserves respect and kindness on the set, from your star to your grip. A good producer creates a sense of security on set. A good producer is open to learning more. If you cannot accept criticism, are unwilling to elicit the help of more experienced producers to join your team, or struggle to make budget or other creative compromises that have the best interest of the film and its eventual success, you will fail.

The above are the most common points that destroy a producer's career before it even starts.

Nobody truly knows the path of a movie once it's made, but you can ensure that your journey to being a working and in-demand producer is a smooth one by avoiding the pitfalls above. In the end, you will have much to gain and will gain the respect of your peers and future partners because of your extensive knowledge, information, people skills, and work ethic.

The job of a producer is tough. It takes perseverance, insight, and some madness as we, the producers, are often the last to get paid adequately for the years of work on any project and are the first to be blamed when a film or TV show falls flat.

Regardless, a good producer has mastered the four things listed below:

You Will Succeed If:

You're a Good Team Leader.

A good producer knows how to inspire his or her team, on set and off, and has a vast knowledge of the process of making a film from the moment the script is chosen to the time the delivery elements are handed on to the distributors.

Always Have a Plan "B".

He or she knows all the possible ways a film or show can be made, can estimate properly the effort and time to be invested in the task at hand, and most of all, is concerned from the beginning on how to make the investors their money back and then some.

You are Humble and Listen to Others.

Unless you are Lorenzo Di Bonaventura or Brian Grazer, there will always be someone who knows more than you. In fact, the greatest producers are the most humble.

You Pay Vendors & Experts During Development.

If you decide to produce a film, be prepared to spend money. And when you do, spend it wisely. It is offensive to ask people to work for free even when you don't have your financing in place. A line producer, casting director, and distribution consultant should be the first to join the team and get paid for their time and experience. If you can't afford their full rates, make them a deal based on deferment, but always pay them something. You can't build a proper building without a good architect, designer, and real estate broker.

The PGA made strict rules on producer credits for movies and who gets to be on stage to pick up the Best Picture Oscar for a reason. I hope this blog will help you understand why.

I leave you with one of my favorite quotes from Lawrence Thurman, producer, and author of the book, So You Want to Be a Producer? is:

"A good producer is a creative person. The top people in the field are creative. But producers do not receive a lot of respect. Go out in the street and stop a dozen strangers and ask what a writer does, what a director does, what an actor does, and you'll get a correct answer. If you ask what a producer does, you'll get a blank look. Nobody knows what we do.

My definition is it's the person who causes the film to be made."

Do you have what it takes to be a producer?

MAKING GOOD USE OF FACT-CHECKING

How do you tap into the power of Information to make the right business choices?

In all Businesses, especially in a creative environment such as the world of Film and Television and Artists, it all starts with a dream. And on the journey to realize your dreams, you will inevitably meet and talk to many people. From them, you will hear either of three things: the truth, the half-truth, and bullshit. As the saying goes "money talks, bullshit walks", it goes even further than this. Developing strong fact-checking skills will save you money, time, and emotional energy as you endeavor to climb up the very tall Hollywood ladder.

Whether you are an artist or a business executive, the goals are the same: to have you and your project be seen and recognized by the right people. Because all our careers are tied to highly creative endeavors, it is normal to "put on a show" to persuade others to give us work, parts, money, and introductions. We are inherently showing an enhanced version of ourselves to attain our goals, and in doing so, we may utilize those "little white lies" to sell ourselves and /or our projects. In principle, there is nothing wrong with that. After all Hollywood is the land of make-believe and lies are almost more common than truths. However, there is a very distinct difference if you are willing to use fact-checking as your secret weapon, in a white lie or a plain old con job.

Even the saying tells it all. Con artist: someone with a certain artistic skill to dupe.

I am here to give you a few common examples of the fine line between white lies, and the more serious consequences of not doing your homework on the people and projects you choose to pursue or give your talents to, or even open your wallet to. This is how I fact-check for my clients and when I need to decide about an actor, a partner, a project, or a vendor I need to pay.

ARE YOU TRULY AN IMDB STAR?

Though a high IMDB star rating may help you get noticed, regardless of your profession, if it is not backed by actual credits and quality and frequency of work, it will backfire. So, when I look at an actor, if I see a high star rating I know that he or she is working on his or her social media. But that is not enough. I will determine the quality and value of the actor based on other factors. Do they have an A-list agent or a very reputable agency representing them? Do they have a solid acting reel online?

Are they movies they have been on festival darlings or Studio films? Do they work frequently and what type of projects do they say yes to? If they name themselves executive producers or producers of their films, what do they do there? Did they bring the money? The IP? Did they work on set? What entitles them to the credit? Are they so busy with their social media presence that they forget to hone their craft? I also check their Facebook, Instagram, and Twitter to get an idea of their personality. Famous or not, I only want "sane" and "professional" people on my sets. Social Media will give me important information about the actors especially when it comes to indie films where I cannot afford to have people who are late on set, party a lot, or have poor people skills.

EVERYBODY IS A PRODUCER

When choosing a producer to set up your script, book, or project, or when seeking a co–producer, it is best to do some fact-checking to find out their experience. It is very easy to get credit as a producer on IMDB. So, I like to go beyond what I see there. I will go online and screen the films or television shows they have produced. This will help me gauge the quality and style of their work. I will reach out to actors they have worked with, even the actors with supporting roles, to get an idea of their roles in the film.

Were they given credit because of a connection or favor? What did they do with the project? Develop it, produce it on set, finance it? Getting on a call with the producer himself or herself will help me determine their level of skill, experience, and connections and if they are a fit for my project or script. I will go beyond IMDB. I will look at their production company website, and their social media imprint, and check them out on Studio System, Variety Insight, etc. I also want to see if they have not produced in a while to find out why. Consummate professionals are always in high demand.

LEGITIMACY OF A PROJECT

A project is as legitimate as the amount of truth it contains. It is fully understood that it makes a big difference if a certain actor or director is interested in the project and if it makes sense, should be name-dropped. It helps in your funding efforts and to validate the value of your material. But there is a fine line between claiming the interest of an actor, director, or distributor or producing a signed piece of paper or confirmation of the reps of such attachment. Once you start making extensive wish lists, and months go by and nothing happens, nobody comes truly on board, the red flags are raised. Once you begin to claim you have distribution and that distribution is a small agreement in Turkey, it raises a red flag. Once you name your film as a big-budget movie yet the writers one has never heard of, or the cast and crew have only been working on micro-budget movies, it raises a red flag. I recently acquired on behalf of my clients a movie with a certain actor attached. When I called the agents to verify his involvement, it was false. The fact the project has not been formally announced to the Trades though it is about to go into production also raises a red flag, especially if there are star actors or directors on board.

A VENDOR THAT TRULY SUPPLIES

When picking your line producer, your DP, your Production designer, your Attorney, or your Distribution representative, what do you truly know about them? Are you still just relying on IMDB credits? If it's a line producer I want to know about the film, they have line produced before mine. If they have only done micro-budget films, it is unlikely they will be the right man or woman for a big-budget movie as they will not be approved by the Bond company. I will want to talk to the producers who hired them before to know if they stayed on budget and if they have a good crew database. The same goes with any crew member, I learned to ask the right questions and apply a lot of the same fact-checking as outlined in the headings before this one.

Finally, my last piece of advice:

Meet everyone you are going to be in bed with, professionally speaking. The Con hides well behind a phone call, an email, or a credit. If you develop good fact-checking skills, you will be able to immediately discern a white lie from a flat-out bullshit job. Character and Professionalism are easily recognized. If you surround yourself with people who embody both, and you represent yourself in the same way, you and your project will shine, like the light of the truth.

HOW DO I SELL MY MOVIE? [AN OBJECTIVE LOOK AT DISTRIBUTION]

So you made a movie. You even have an offer from a sales agent to sell it worldwide.
You are excited.
Your film is selling in Cannes!
It's selling at the American Film Market!
It's screening at Berlinale.

You're having viewing parties with friends and family, showing off the brochure, or listing your movie in the Trades. You dream about the new movie you will make or the house you'll buy with the profits from the first one, and you're sure there will be so many dollars coming your way from the sales of your film and after your investors are paid off.

Then the months go by.
Your phone isn't ringing.
And when you call your sales agent to get a revenue report, you get crickets from the other side.

The global marketplace is constantly changing and every country your sales agent is attempting to market your movie to has its own set of needs and is always in flux. What's more, the competition is fierce, as there is more supply than demand for the traditional distribution model.

As the representative of several international distributors, I have the advantage of being on the "other side," observing what works and what doesn't. I get to understand how buyers think and react to the films sold in the marketplace. as well as what makes them open their checkbooks.

If you're struggling to sell a film, here are some of the more common reasons you're hitting the wall with the sale of your film:

Your Movie is Too Short or Too Long.

Your film should sit at a pretty 89 to 105 minutes. If your film is closer to 83 minutes, it's way too short. Certain territories need a minimum of 86 minutes WITHOUT END CREDITS to consider acquiring your film. Other territories will not release movies that are longer than two hours unless your film is the next installment of a Marvel franchise or the work of an Oscar director like Martin Scorsese.

Your Movie Looks Cheap.
"Made with a shoestring budget" is the kiss of death in the world of sales. Even if your movie was produced on credit card debt and donations from friends and family, with crews and actors working for basically free, it needs to "feel and look" big and expensive in its scope. Buyers have a trained eye and can tell right away if the film was produced cheaply. Their thought will be that you truly do not love your project, as otherwise, you would have waited to have it produced for the right budget.

Your Movie is Too Depressing.
In today's world, there's a lot out there that can depress us. From politics to climate change to economic crisis, movies that deal with the lowest common denomination of humanity where every scene is tragic and the ending is so hopeless and disturbing that it makes you want to slash your wrists, will not make a distributor open eager to show it in his territory. Exceptions are made for certain filmmakers who are considered auteurs and films that have major festival recognition.

Your Movie has an Expiration Date.
Sadly, a movie shot two to three years ago that just got picked up for distribution - is considered dated and old. Buyers only pick up films in post-production or just completed. After six months in the market, the title is considered unsellable.

Your Film Lacks Social Media Attention.
Unfortunately, a sales agent will not pay for your PR or be your PR or Social Media champion. It's up to you to do the work. This means that when you make a film, you have to simultaneously build an audience for it on all social media platforms. Work to generate coverage with bloggers and magazines, too. Buyers check social media assets with a simple

Google search before deciding if the film is worth acquiring. If your film has no web presence, it will have no market presence either.

Your "Stars" Aren't Sellable.
Unless your film wins awards and has a huge social media buzz behind it, a project with no notable cast has poor chances of being sold. And what you consider a "name" may not be a name in any country you are planning to sell. For example, Eric Roberts, Michael Madsen, and Seth Green may be A-list actors to you, but they won't sell your film. This has nothing to do with their acting talent, but everything to do with the fact that they've been cast in way too many C-level films.

You Have the Wrong Cast for Your Genre.
Putting a comedy actor in a horror film will not sell. Unless it's someone like Adam Sandler and even then, it's a challenge. There have been very few actors who have been able to cross over to other genres. Everyone knows who Stallone is, and he's associated with action movies. To put Stallone in a dramatic family piece will most likely tank the movie.

You've Gone to Too Many Festivals.
Submitting your movie to dozens of festivals will cheapen it. Much like someone who sleeps with every person they go on a date with, you'll bring the movie to a point where no one will want it. You need to be very specific about your festival strategy. Don't go to small festivals unless you've exhausted the big ones. Have a few good laurels on your poster, but do not plaster it with them. A buyer will immediately think 'art house,' which will make it unsellable. You may also be viewed as desperate. I know you want to see audiences applaud you for your work, but I think it's more important to see yourself paying back your investors so they can fund your next movie.

You Have the Wrong Sales Agent.
If your movie is an action-adventure and you give it to a sales agent who specializes in drama and comedy, they don't have the right kind of buyers. If your movie is a TV movie or market-specific and you're lucky enough to give it to a sales agency that handles A list of theatrical movies, they won't put the same work or passion into selling your film. At the most, it will just be a negotiating tool to sell the bigger film or a filler title.

Having said all of this, don't lose hope, my friends. There is a way to turn things around and start earning dollars to repay you for your sacrifices and the months or years of hard work you put in to get your film from script to screen. Not all of the instances above can be fixed, but you can change the buyer's mind or shift their perception.

If you are still in post-production and your film is about to go to the marketplace, here are some Tips to Move Things in the Right Direction:

Re-edit your film. If it's too long, get an expert to give you notes from a global marketplace storytelling perspective and hire a great editor to do magic. If it's too short, raise a little bit of cash and add a few scenes. This could help you increase your production value, too. If you need to add scenes, don't make them "talky." Make them emotionally charged or visually stunning. Both can be accomplished with good actors and a great DP.

Make your movie look more expensive. Here is your chance to have a great DP or VFX artist help you with a powerful and easy tool: LOCATION LOCATION LOCATION. (Natural or artificial.)

If your movie is "old" by distribution standards, then self-distribute. at least in U.S. platforms. This will automatically change the IMDb date on your listing, as it will go by the date of release.

Get busy writing to bloggers who are fans of your genre. Ask them to see the movie, review it, and share it on social media. Pay them, if necessary. Find an influencer to do an Insta story from a screening at a festival. Get into some movie buff chat rooms and stir up a conversation. THE DEVIL INSIDE became a box office hit because the filmmakers would enter chat rooms and talk about the existence of the devil while asking for comments and thoughts. This generated a buzz. Use buzzwords, hashtags, and keywords to bring your movie title up on Google. Compliment other filmmakers on their movies and throw your movie's name into the conversation if it's similar to theirs.

Recast and reshoot your film during the editing process. If you're confident with your script and story, hire a casting director to pay good money to a marketable actor. That actor doesn't have to be an A-lister but should be someone with a strong social media presence or the star of a successful TV show. Film them for a few days and throw them in your film. Give them a producer credit and part of the back end if necessary. That will motivate them.

If your sales agent doesn't have a clear strategy for how to sell your film, do not sign. If they are acquiring too many movies and you are one of a dozen, do not sign. If they give you a 10-year contract and no information on how they will make your movie matter or stand the test of time beyond the first year of the markets, do not sign.

Unfortunately, there is no immediate solution to unusual casting. I would suggest you "spin" your story about the cast and work on the social media universe to convince your audience that your cast choices were, indeed, brilliant. The studios did that with Jim Carrey and Adam Sandler, for example. Granted, they had marketing dollars, and the actors promoted the films and were damn good in their roles.

Perhaps with enough buzz, the buyers will also see it too.

I look forward to seeing you and celebrating your success at future Cannes, Toronto, Berlin, Sundance, Venice, Tribeca, AFI, and so on. Never give up. There is always plenty of time to get it right.

2020 VISION: MAKING NEW YEAR'S RESOLUTIONS STICK FOR YOUR CREATIVE GOALS

The holidays are the perfect opportunity to take inventory of all the activities you have done this year and examine what has worked for you and what you need to improve on.

A Resolution is only as good as the plan devised to execute it.

And before the planning, comes the soul searching. Every activity we undertake in this life, be it professional or personal, has an opportunity for growth at its core.

I am offering below some questions you may want to ask yourself that will show you what your top 5 priorities should be for your script, project, or film and some of my personal recommendations and practical suggestions for the areas that you have decided, on after careful examination, that contains the most of your weak spots.

How are your pitching skills?

If you know who your ICA (Ideal Client Avatar) is and what emotion you need to convey to solicit a read or an in-person meeting, you are ahead of the game.

If you can write a query email that states who you are, the comps of your project or script, and gives just enough information on the story and plot to incite interest, you are ahead of the game.

If you can sit in a room or get on the phone with an interested party and be able to establish a genuine connection (knowing the person you are pitching to and making a personal compliment stick does go a long way) while being able to convey your passion and the most important elements of your story in less than 5 minutes, you are ahead of the game.

For some great tips in how to "sell", I would suggest you read "Born to Win" by Zig Ziglar.

What is the positive-to-negative feedback ratio you have received so far?

If you have gotten at least 70% response to your queries or meetings and script submissions regardless of the reaction, you are ahead of the game. You made enough of an impression for an executive to take the time to let you know they did read you or thought of your project and therefore were able to respond in some manner.

If you had a polite pass, such as a compliment on some aspect of your story and writing, or a pass with actual details on why your material was passed on, you are ahead of the game.

If you have a response for you to keep in touch with the progress of your project or script, you are ahead of the game.

If your feedback ratio is under 70%, then bluntly put, your material is just not good enough or its time for the current marketplace has not come.

For some great tips on making some improvements to your material, I would suggest the book "Your Screenplay Sucks: 100 Ways to make it great" by William M. Akers

How much time have you spent this year honing your craft and getting up-to-date information and knowledge on how the Business works?

If you read an average of 10 produced screenplays a year, you are ahead of the game. Brownie points out for being able to recognize why those scripts got made, to begin with – if it was the technical writing, the sum of its creative attachments, or the message aka emotional core of the material.

If you watch at least the Pilot of every hit show out there at least the top 10 box office hits of the year and the top 10 indie films (hit as defined by critics, word of mouth), you are ahead of the game.

Information is power.

If you read the Trades every day (Variety, Hollywood Reporter) and can with confidence name at least one credit for the top Show Runners or Hollywood Producers or A-list stars, you are ahead of the game. Brownie points out that if you know the history behind how a certain show got greenlit or the journey of a hit or Oscar-winning film to get realized.

For opportunities to attend screenings of some wonderful indie films and shows, you may want to consider joining Film Independent.

How many Industry execs have you met in person or had ongoing communications with this past year?

Networking is the single most important thing you can focus on to advance your career. A while ago I wrote in one of my blogs about the power behind the power lunch. If you have succeeded in inviting to lunch or coffee or drinks an established actor, director, producer, distributor, or financier, you are ahead of the game.

There are things you can do to cultivate and nourish those relationships and believe it or not, none of those things have to do with the quality of your material (well, partially they do) and everything to do with your personality and genuine interest in getting to know the people you want to be in business with.

Do you have any limiting beliefs or do you self-sabotage?

Succeeding at anything in life is a mental game. If you are not at a peak mental state, it is hard to follow through or get results from the activities in the 4 paragraphs above.

If you are dedicating at least 20 minutes of your day to priming – meaning being in a prime high-vibration state, you are ahead of the game. An upbeat attitude is contagious and will open more doors than an impersonal query blast. Much of it can be attained with meditation, self-help books, listening to upbeat music, being in nature, and following a good diet and fitness regime.

If you have taken critique well and are open to improving your craft or doing whatever is necessary to show your love for your work and the love for the Business you chose to be in, you are ahead of the game.

If by reading this you have recognized patterns that deter you from your goals, work on these first as you embark on the New Year and make them a Resolution.

If you have recognized regular routines that have already been implemented and have yielded positive results, keep going! And increase 5x.

I promise you that getting these 5 questions properly answered will create natural action steps to make your New Year's resolutions stick.

I leave you with a great quote by Paul Arden, a former executive at Saatchi & Saatchi and a legend of British advertising.

> *"What is a good idea? One that happens is. If it doesn't, it isn't".*

The best piece of advice ever given was by the art director of Harper's Bazaar told Richard Avedon, one of the world's greatest photographers.

The advice was simple. *"Astonish Me!"* Bear those words in mind and you will be a success. Happy New Year!

INSIDE THE MIND OF A DISTRIBUTOR- THE THINKING PROCESS BEFORE THE ACQUISITION OF A PROJECT OR FILM.

For many years the second most needed element for any movie or project to be successful, outside of a Studio deal, was the Sales Agent.

There have been many theories and speculations on the process of getting a sales agent on board a film, TV series, or project. A lot of it was answered broadly the necessity of a finance plan, talent attachments, and a good script.

However, in today's world, which has ALL the power is the Territorial Distributor. Having an A-List sales agent means very little these days, especially now when Television and Film Markets, as well as major Festivals, are being scrapped due to this pandemic.

For this reason, I wanted to give you a sneak- peek at the thinking process of major international distributors and the incredibly vital role they play in the survival of the Film and Television business.

I have the privilege of representing 11 major THEATRICAL distributors in key international territories. As a result, I am the eyes and ears of global trends and buying patterns that are constantly changing and becoming even more challenging.

Let me first debunk a myth about sales agents.

Sales Agents do not finance a film, primarily. If they have a track record, they are likely to finance (partially) a film because they can rely upon a certain number of territorial distributors to commit to any given project they are selling in a Market or Festival. For some sales agents, they even have output partnerships meaning that they have one preferred distributor they deal with on a specific territory that buys all their contents, sight unseen as long as it fits certain credentials.

If no buyer signs a licensing deal for any given film, the film, unless bought out worldwide by a Studio or a Major Streaming platform is dead in the water.

The second myth I want to debunk for you is.

Sales projections mean NOTHING. They can possibly be an indicator of a hopeful performance of a film, but almost every single time, these projections are given to a producer to pacify their equity investors and to convince a Producer to sign with YXZ Sales Agent.

The process of evaluation of a buyer is different according to the Territory and Rights being acquired.

But below are some of the most common questions that are being asked by a Buyer.

Is this Film or Project going to pass censorship in any given Country? Some Territories, for example, will not release films that are overtly violent or have LGBT storylines.

Is this Film or Project getting the US Release and in which manner? Having a platform release in the US shuts off some territorial deals in some countries such as the Middle East, whereas once a film is seen on Netflix is pirated and therefore useless and of no value for acquisition. If the US Release is of a theatrical nature, then the Distributor, the P&A, and the number of theatres it is getting the release in also play a factor in the acquisition process.

Is the story or subject matter of appeal in my Territory? Some countries abhor non-physical comedy, for example, so you can have a US Comedy with A-list stars and will still not get acquired.

Does the script get good coverage? ALL Theatrical Buyers, before even tracking a project for Territorial Acquisition get it covered by their Reps such as yours truly. Or by a Team of Trusted Readers (not online coverage companies). Submitting a project with coverage from an online coverage company means nothing as such coverage does not consider elements needed for the buyers to understand the value of the material.

Does the Project Film have a set delivery date that will be kept? All Buyers need to have specific dates of Delivery of the film. Delay in delivery will cause cancellation of any Agreements and non-payment of the Minimum Guarantee.

Is the Project Film in the hands of a Sales Agency or Representative that the Buyers has already done business with? As a Buyer's rep, we never buy from Companies or Executives who have not had a long and stellar track record in the International Sales arena.

Who is the team? - If the Film or Project is in the pre-finance stage, Buyers will ask to see the budget, verifiable attachments, and a reputable lender. This is because when a bankable Buyer buys a film, they are liable to pay for it even if the film turns out to be a total disaster with no negotiation or reduction of price as the Buyer's agreement has been used for borrowing from a Lender to finance the Film or Project.

Is the Film or Project properly cast and with a solid marketing plan in place? Every country has different talent tiers. What a producer mistakenly thinks is an A-lister maybe a C-lister in several major territories. As a Buyer, we cross-check the performance of every actor in the territories we handle as well as Social Media imprints.

This is just a small segment of a very long process that goes through a buyer's mind before pulling the trigger of signing a deal for any given film or project. Other elements are who reasonable or unreasonable asking prices are and of course, the current release trends that change literally every 3 months. For that reason, if a film or project is not sold in major territories within the first six months of being in the marketplace, chances are it will not sell at all.

The Buyers aka Territorial distributors have been burned one time too many by overpaying for films or investing in projects that turned out poorly or never got off the ground. Having the finger in the pulse of the Buyers is even more important than securing a Sales Agent. At the same time, a Buyer interacts on relationships primarily so as a writer, filmmaker, or producer, it is unlikely you will be able to form a true bond with a Buyer without the alliance of a Sales Agent or someone who can open those doors for you, who has the authority and the trust of the Buyer. By the same token, when I am looking at the interests of my Buyer clients, I will also at times explore new alliances directly with producers who have a solid track record.

As Sales Agents tend to try to sell more than one picture at a time, pushing often for the acquisition of more than one project to get the project or film my clients want, it has become almost acceptable to take a chance in acquiring directly from a producer or production company. In that case, many of the same points covered above are taken into consideration.

I firmly believe that despite the emergence of the power of global buyouts of a movie or project, there is nothing like nurturing a film that is being handled and released country by country and seeing the joy in the faces of my clients, who buy truly because they love the cinematic experience of a film when they have indeed chosen well and the film becomes a hit in their own country, regardless of US box office performance.

As a producer, I have never been so humbled as when I am working as a Buyer's rep, which is my constant and only source of inspiration to create and help see content made that will be enjoyed across cultures and borders.

I hope you will think of Buyers, not Sales Agents when you make your next film. They are the end of the delivery line and the assurance of your investors to break even and hope to profit.

GOT SOUL?

On Christmas Day, the Disney/Pixar animated film SOUL was released on the Disney Plus platform.

It is possibly one of the greatest and most impactful Disney films made to date. If you have not seen the film yet, be warned of the Spoiler Alerts that must be revealed for me to outline the five most important takeaways that will reframe the saying *"it's the little things"* into what I would say call the simple way to live life to the fullest.

Soul tells the story of Joe Gardner (Jamie Foxx), a middle school band teacher and aspiring jazz musician who for one too many years has been trying to have a career from his passion. By the hand of destiny, he books the gig of his dreams, and on the way to his first performance has an accident and ends in a coma. You are probably wondering how this is even made for kids and families.

Yet, in exploring what happens when we die, we discover the magic beauty, and grace of living. When Joe is sent to The Great Before, the place where young souls (actual souls) are being prepared for their trip to Earth where they will be born as humans, he is given an assignment, that if he succeeds, will allow him to return to his body. His task is to guide SOUL number 22 (22), to find her unique "spark", so that she may be sent to Earth.

22, has been afraid of life on Earth and refuses to leave this in-between world. Her theory is that most souls inhabiting their Earth start with enthusiasm and wonder only to find their dreams crushed. Who would want to live there?

This unlikely friendship between a human whose life got cut short and a soul who does not want to become human becomes the conduit for five simple yet profound life lessons that many of us forgot, especially during 2020.

In a year as tumultuous as the last one, it's easy to feel as if the world is weighing us down. It's easy to feel like a lost soul going through the motions of everyday life, losing sight of the little things in front of us every minute of the day.

Let the five core themes of SOUL act as a flashlight to guide you.

FIND THE SPARK IN EVERYTHING. "I was born to do this" is what Joe keeps telling everyone when it comes to his playing music. Do we truly have one single purpose? I was born to do this. This is one of the most important lines we tell ourselves and the world when we want to accomplish our most coveted dream. It is the feeling of "being in the zone", something we experience when doing what we believe we were born, our special talent, and it cannot be compared to anything else but pure ecstasy. Joe continued to pursue his dream because of his obsession that he was born to be a musician. However, in the Great Before, the "Spark" is that moment when souls have acquired their unique gifts and character traits and are ready to be sent to Earth to live. What we were born to do, all of us is to LIVE this great adventure of being human, with its joys and sorrows. It's the journey, not the destination that matters. It is hard for us to accept changes in the future that we might have hoped to go differently. But with time, we can try to accept where life takes us and maybe start to feel fulfilled regardless.

STOP GETTING LOST IN THE HUSTLE. Relentlessly pursuing a dream can be exhausting and stressful. Forcing things and stressing over finding our worth in the recognition of our talent can be extremely stressful. The daily pressure to survive, to make a name for ourselves, and to chase our goals, makes us forget the blessings we have, regardless of the wealth, fame, or success in the conventional sense. Life is made of small moments such as the joy of eating pizza, a gust of wind caressing our faces, getting lost in the notes played by a street musician, and so much more.

A WORD FROM YOUR MOUTH CAN CHANGE A PERSON FOREVER. We do not have to be teachers by profession to make an impact on another. We are all mentors. When Joe has a meeting with one of his students, who has been bullied and feels worthless, he pays her one single compliment. And that's where we see the power of words. A moment of kindness and understanding can change in an instant the life trajectory and destiny of another person. This is where the principle of "we are all one" is best demonstrated. This also applies to negative words as well, that can cut deeper than a knife.

ALL DREAMS ARE WORTHY. Joe is so busy pursuing his dream, obsessively talking about it to everyone he knows, that he forgets to listen. In one special moment, he is at the barber shop getting a haircut and hears as if for the first time about his barber's passion for owning his store and serving his customers by shaving them. What seems like a meaningless task for one person, can be another's personal triumph and joy. In the film, they call it being in the "in-between", that place where time and space are in suspension as we are fully absorbed by the pleasure of doing what we love the most.

ALL WE HAVE IS NOW. Life is amazing. And it can end in a moment. What will be remembered about when it's all over? Soul is a love letter to the gift of being alive, to learn to appreciate the highs and the lows, and the people who cross our path. If we just step into our memories and look at all the special moments that we had in our and were not present for them because of being so stressed trying to do something different.

The purpose of life is to live it. We must not waste one single minute of it. I cried when I saw the film like a baby as I faced how fragile all of us are in our mortality.

I truly hope this gem of a film wins the Oscar for Best Animation but most of all I am grateful for the souls who had the imagination and heart to create such a powerful yet simple story that can impact children and adults alike with a newfound appreciation of "the little things".

Note: You can watch the film in its entirety on Disney+.

PLAYING CHESS WITH LIFE

Nothing is more powerful than word of mouth. A very original NETFLIX series called THE QUEEN'SGAMBIT, became a surprise hit for the streaming giant in 2020.

The Queen's Gambit is about the rise to fame of an orphan chess prodigy, Beth Harmon, during her quest to become the world's greatest chess player in the 1950s and 1960s, while struggling with emotional problems and drug and alcohol dependency.

Beyond the incredible slick visuals and stellar performances, it ultimately drew people into a world of strategic thinking and awakened in its viewers a newfound passion for the game of chess, which in so many ways could be defined as the game of life.

Chess is a very challenging mental game but has at its core some very profound yet simple principles for navigating our daily existence and challenges.

After the pandemic and months of isolation, we are back to the business of living and interacting with other humans, even virtually, therefore it has become more than ever essential to brush up on some strategy skills to master one's life and the principles of chess are a great resource.

These are 5 takeaways from this emotional and intoxicating series, which we can all implement to master our emotions and future.

- **Be the chess player, not the chess piece.**
On the board of life, you can either be moving against the director of the pressure points and exterior situations, or you can be looking at life as a journey with a finite destination, which in chess is called "THE END GAME". We have the power to decide to make moves that will empower us and take us there, being vigilant of what obstacles may intend to overcome them.

- **Chess is not about psychology. It is about good movies.**
Ultimately, emotions are not something to be ashamed of, neither are our inner demons. Though how we play the game of life can be recognized by our physiology, our destiny is not ruled by our psychology as much as by a series of good moves.

- **We learn as much about the games we lose as the games that we win.**
Sometimes we have to fail many times to gain perspective on our weaknesses and our innate natural resilience. Making an inventory of what works and what needs fine-tuning allows us to confront ourselves calmly and analytically and prepare for the next move. Sometimes taking a step backward will help us take better steps forward in life.

- **All the pawns on your side of the board matter.**
Ultimately you are the King or Queen of your existence. Just like in chess, life is not a solitary game. You cannot be Queen or King to none. You have others on the journey with you, and you give them the level of importance on your side of the board according to how much or how little they contribute to your life. If we do not have a group to shield us protect us or go into battle with us during the difficult moments, it will be very easy for the Queen or the King to be taken down.

- **One single move can change everything.**
The overall theme in fact in The Queen's Gambit was that Beth tried every single move in her head to predict the outcome before she even played. Thinking ahead was her way to gain control of her mind and also to manage the chaos around her life. She did that analytically and when it came down to playing her biggest competitor, it was one single move that moved her Queen to the other side of the game to checkmate.

When was the last time you wrote your life rules?

I have added those guideposts, as I call them, to my Hollywood toolkit and they have come in handy on multiple occasions.

And that is the beauty and the power of meaningful storytelling in film and television.

BONUS CHAPTERS

- The Studio Writer with Evan Spiliotopoulos.
- Wrangling Cats with Jay Russell.
- With an Open Hand with DeeDee Pfeiffer.

My next book will be available 2025 - learn more about my journey in Hollywood and my honest and heartfelt conversations with true Hollywood Insiders, powerhouses, and Thought Leaders.

Sign up for exclusive private coaching with Alexia to prepare for what could potentially become the most pivotal meeting of your life.

Make sure you're fully equipped and primed for success.

POWER HOUR- CREATIVE COACHING
https://www.alexia-melocchi.com/coaching

LET'S CONNECT!

www.alexia-melocchi.com
www.littlestudiofilms.com
https://www.youtube.com/@AlexiaMelocchi/videos
https://www.instagram.com/alexiamelocchireal
https://www.tiktok.com/@aleciamelocchi

THE STUDIO WRITER
with EVAN SPILIOTOPOULOS.

"I write to give myself strength. I write to be the characters that I am not. I write to explore all the things that I am afraid of." - Joss Whedon

In this chapter, I am talking with Evan Spiliotopoulos, a very in-demand screenwriter, who has been writing nonstop since the late 90s. From Greece, he has worked with every major studio in Hollywood. He started in animation where he wrote for Disney Studios, The Little Mermaid and Tinkerbell before he continued to write Snow White and the Huntsman and the latest live-action Beauty and the Beast. Most recently, he wrote horror such as The Pope's Exorcist with Russell Crowe.

Of course, I had to ask Evan – how do one go from animation to action to fairy tale fantasy to horror?

"Recently the wonderful writer Craig Mazin, who co-wrote The Huntsman with me, the sequel to Snow White and the Huntsman, has received a ton of acclaim for writing the two great HBO shows Chernobyl and now The Last of Us. Craig started in comedies such as the sequels to The Hangover. And a lot of people now are standing back and going: Oh, my God, what a pivot. How do you go from all these kinds of complete slapstick comedies to these two really serious emotional shows?

But you cannot typecast writers.

Stephen King, one of his most wonderful books is a baseball drama. And you can pick a genre that you love - like I love fairy tales. But that doesn't mean we can't write Action, Horror, fantasy period pieces, dramas, or all that. What it comes down to is a writer writes about characters, the canvas could be anything, as long as you have a character that you believe in, really love, and feel like you've developed."

\#

I also believe that characters are more important than the story. Because you could have a great story that if it has no characters you are not gonna get invested in it. And I would also add it's also about themes. When I spoke with another well-known writer on my show, his reply was: you want to start with this as a story about a man or a woman who… and you want to go and draw two common themes. And I will think that even in horror, although I don't watch a lot of it, there's got to be some character work going in there, right?

"If it's great horror, absolutely! I mean, Hereditary is a character piece. The Exorcist is a character piece, both for the Greek priests played by Jason Miller. Ellen Bernstein and her daughter, it's the only way horror becomes relatable, frightening, and engaging is if you care about the characters, and you relate and recognize the characters.

By the way, a really quick point, the writer that you were mentioning is absolutely right. But the character is the plot. So the idea is that if you're following a character under a set of circumstances that provide a theme, the story is going to be around that person's experiences. So even if it's James Bond with eight set pieces, you're still following a character on a journey."

\#

What Evan mentions is true in any story, but I wanted to take a step back and learn more about Evan's story. How does a nice boy from Greece, move to America – did you go "Mom, Dad, I want to be a writer?" What did they say? "Are you crazy?"

"Well, the circumstances were a little bit particular, because by the time I graduated high school, I had lost my dad. And my mom was American. I wanted to come to the United States to study, and she was supportive of that.

I think that made a very big difference for me, obviously, because a lot of young people in Greece want to leave the country, but can't because of family circumstances - because it's expensive, because it's a risk, and what kind of career are you really going to pursue? I have to say upfront that I was in a unique position where my mom was fully supportive. So I moved to the States.

And in my undergraduate years, I just fell in love with film. I mean, from a little kid I was already in love with film, but I fell in love with film studies. I got a degree, an undergraduate degree in film theory, which is very surprisingly helpful because what film theory is; you watch a ton of movies going back to the silent era. And that gives you a context of how this art form has evolved. How stories are told, that a lot of people who just think of the movies began with Star Wars don't understand.

Then I went to Washington, DC to American University and got a master's degree in screenwriting, which I will say: a good screenwriting master's degree is completely useless. All you have to do is download the American Film Institute, its top 100 screenplays of all time, read them, and you've saved your money and you've gotten an education on how to write screenplays. I then moved to LA and I was lucky enough that my writing samples got me assignments, and it all kind of started happening."

#

I'm a huge advocate of downloading all the scripts again, either nominated or box office hits as I'm sure there is a formula there, and for everyone to learn – writers and producers.

"Formula? It absolutely is. But of course, the challenge and the creative aspect of it is how do you take something that is a formula and make it feel fresh in you, and break the formula and restructure it and use it to your advantage in a surprising way? That's the challenge."

Every writer that I know is struggling to get represented by a manager or an agent of sorts. I wanted to know more about how Evan was able to get his representation. Did he have to get his first writing assignment, or go out and sell his script on his own? Or was he lucky enough to get someone in his corner early on?

"Excellent question. And I have the magic answer. The magic answer is you get a lawyer, you get an entertainment lawyer because you're going to need an entertainment lawyer. An entertainment lawyer does not go via a screening process like the agent of the manager is going to look at you and scrutinize you and re-write samples, and rightly so. And if you're not a name, and if you're just starting out, you have to really blow their socks off.

An entertainment lawyer won't do any of those things. You're just going to hire them. And they're going to work for you, you know, project by project, but they know agents and managers. When you're a baby writer and all you're gonna get is option agreements, the likelihood of selling a million-dollar spec screenplay is astronomical. And if it happens, you're gonna get an agent or manager and it's exactly what happened to me."

#

As a writer, you have to have a lot of passion and make a lot of sacrifices, because you're not necessarily going to be a millionaire overnight. Learning more about Evan's journey, I am asking him a two-prong question. So were you supporting yourself with writing assignments? What was the thing that was helping you continue writing the things that you care about the most and what kind of stories do you want to tell?

"The first prong is my assignments supported me as a writer, but I have to tell you, I moved to LA 95. And I had the good fortune right away of getting to Sci-Fi Channel movies. At the time, when they were doing the monster of the month, I think it was where they were basically doing at the most a million dollars. And that was about it. And the movies are awful, but you got your IMDB credit, you patted the resume, and you got to produce a screenplay, and that makes you look good.

However, it reached a point when those movies don't support it, you don't feed you really. And the point when I had I think $3,000 in my bank account, which to live in LA at the time back in the late 90s was maybe squeezing it three months of life.

And so I was already starting to figure out okay, I'm not going back. But what kind of part-time job can I get that will also help me give me the time to write? That's when Disney hired me. And that changed everything. I was at Disney for eight years. And at that point, once Disney approves you, even if it's Disney tunes, you're in with a studio that massive has given you its stamp. Now you're okay to be known to other studios. So that was that was that aspect of it.

The second one was what projects interest me. So the thing is, there isn't a specific I wish I could tell you, boy, I always wanted to do the story of Jane Eyre. There's not that there's not a particular theme or project or concept that hooks me.

It's always character. When I directed my first movie during the pandemic, what I loved about it was that it was about a broken journalist who was caught his earlier in his career fabricating stories, and it ruined him and threw him down to National Enquirer-type levels. And then he finds these real miracles. He believes they're going to resurrect his career and put him on the map again. And then he discovers that he's opened Pandora's box. In order to shut it he has to destroy himself. And for me, that was an interesting character.

That was a huge journey. So it just always goes back to character ."

#

Evan directed THE UNHOLY. And I wanted to know how it was for Evan to go from writing to directing.

"It was terrifying! And I didn't want to do it. It was just circumstances that landed on me because when you speak to nine to ten people in LA nine of them will say I want to direct.

And it just happened that there was a book by a late great English horror novelist named James Herbert that I read when I was 13 years old. We won't say when. But when I was 13 years old, at the time I was in Greece, obviously growing up and I knew this was a movie. I was already a film buff. So I felt it was Billy Wilder's Ace in the Hole meets The Exorcist.

My name started getting stronger and stronger, my career started taking off, and I would go around to the studios that liked me and basically ask them to adopt this orphan child for me to write. And finally, Screen Gems, which is the genre division of Sony, in 2019, jumped aboard but they had an edict of hiring A-list writers, I'm making air quotes with my fingers, who never directed, who wanted to directly surround them with a team that could help them. We just know how to tell it on paper and given that shot, and so my entire team basically said yes for me, so they threw me off the deep end.

And what got me through? Sam Raimi- he was our producer. Sam's awesome and he held my hand. But the thing that I have to underline is we shot it during the pandemic. Not intentionally, obviously. So we started shooting in February of 2020. We were supposed to shoot for seven weeks, we shut down on week four, all of us came home, we edited remotely the footage then we had waited until mid- September, when Massachusetts opened up again, with very strict regulations to face the absolute nightmare of having to shoot during those regulations, which was, by the way, totally understandable, because they were far on safety. And I only use the term nightmare in terms of production nightmare.

But it was basically like you couldn't have more than nine extras in a room and they couldn't be sitting next to each other. And we had a funeral scene to film. So we had to get a second unit to shoot those nine extras 100 times, dress them in different clothes, and move them to different parts of the church. And then when we assembled it, these nine extras were the entire congregation. And of course, there were the physical things off I was in a hazmat suit the whole time.

September in Massachusetts is no longer fall, it's summer. And we went from shooting in minus-one temperatures to shooting in 100-degree temperatures. I was lobster red every single day."

#

That situation is insane. And it brings to mind my friend who was a TV producer who found himself constrained to a hotel while accustomed to being hands-on on set. Despite wanting to engage with actors and offer support, the circumstances limited him to virtual interactions via Zoom. It was a significant challenge. On a different note, some filmmakers opt for secluded ranches, quarantining with a small crew to create movies, and handling everything from cameras to crew work collectively.

Regarding the studio system, there have been infamous tales about the ordeal of working with studios, inundated with notes from numerous executives, constantly changing. And I have a few of the stories myself. Is that still the norm, or has there been some improvement in managing this chaos?

"I will tell you this, it is absolutely 100 sets of notes from 100 Different executives. But I've never felt that that was necessarily an awful experience. Because I haven't been in a situation where the notes are insane. And I'm sure that happens. I just haven't seen it. So you know, in the studio level when 50, 100, 150, 200, $250 million are at play, there is a large degree of scrutiny.

And here's the quid pro quo of studio versus an indie studio. In the studio world, they will be breathing down your neck. I'd like to say the Eye of Sauron would be upon you at any given time. In the indie world, you have mostly total freedom to do whatever you want. However, the alternative is, that the studio is going to make your movie go theatrical, and your movie is going to be seen and your movie is gonna get a good streaming deal and your movies gonna get all these other perks and good publicity and all that kind of stuff. In the independent world, there is a pretty good chance your movie will never be seen by anyone.

Now, the only thing that is that I can tell you upfront that is problematic with the studio system - there are a lot of writers on a movie, and that often leads to a situation where the script feels like it's been created by a committee"

#

Multiple writers often create a complex dynamic where decisions regarding credits, hierarchy, shared acknowledgment, and financial compensation arise. Sometimes you may have a great TV pilot written by a relatively unknown writer who will not see the light of day unless a showrunner writer comes on board. This is a point I've emphasized to some of my clients: the willingness to relinquish credit for the sake of fostering creativity and potentially transforming a project into a household name, like "The Walking Dead," credited to its creators. I believe being recognized as the creator holds more significance than being labeled solely as a screenwriter, and this is something Evan also agrees with.

But what happens when you have pitched the story of yours and they say We want to take the story, but we want to have somebody else write it?

"It has not happened to me. I will tell you why though. It's because, by the time I was in the position to go into studios and pitch my stories, I already had a name. So there would be no point in swapping me out because they would only swap me out with someone at my level."

And this brings me to my next topic. As a producer, I see the market from a producer perspective. But how does that look like for Evan and the screenwriters - are scripts getting optioned anymore, or is it a different landscape?

"I have not optioned anything in over a decade and a half. Options are usually where you're a baby writer.

And it's not a studio that's involved. It's a producer, who likes your script and wants to take a crack at it.

I've never seen a studio say we'll option something: a studio will option a book when they've got a deal going on. And they won't just buy the book outright, they'll option a book because they will have a writer who did a take. And then if the writer's script is great, you get the movie made, then they exercise the option in the book, but I've never heard of them optioning a script, that's a producer thing."

Following up on what Evan is talking about - in essence when a studio hires you to write, it's comparable to a step deal. The studio provided the source material, requesting your attempt at it—drafting the initial version. If it gets approved for production, the arrangement shifts, but they ensure you're fully compensated as a writer for your work on the script rather than just an option.

"Well, if it's a novel, the novelist will own the IP (intellectual property) until the option gets exercised. So they'll get paid whatever they get paid to put their script book on the shelf for the studio to green-lit to develop a screenplay.

And then if the screenplay gets green-lit and is getting made, the studio will then exercise their option to fully buy the book, in which case now they own the IP.

But if the film doesn't get made, the option expires, and the IP reverts back to the Creator, who is the novelist. "

#

I learned about a recently deceased well-known director who encountered issues with a studio. Despite the studio not utilizing the intellectual property, reclaiming the rights became challenging due to the obscene costs involved. It's important to make sure that any project, be it a script or a book, will happen within a specific timeframe. If not, like Evan just mentioned – it can be shelved indefinitely.

Regarding experiences as a writer, have there been instances where a movie idea was created, and shortly after, someone else seemingly wrote something strikingly similar? How does someone protect themselves from such situations?

"There is something called the collective subconscious, which is the stuff that inspires you to write that particular screenplay, other people are watching at the same time, other people are absorbing that at the same time.

So before you get upset that I got robbed, you have to be sure that there was a chain of contact where this other person who wrote a similar thing was somehow exposed to your idea or exposed to your script.

You can sue for whatever reason, but you can't hope to win anything unless you can prove that you got robbed."

What about people working with books, is there better protection there? I feel that people are doing a lot more pre-existing IP, whether it's a comic book or book, a short story, or a remake because it adds a level of protection. Have you found that to be true?

"I think it definitely adds a layer of protection. But I think the 80% reason that they're doing that is because that pre-existing IP already comes with a core group of fans and has had some publicity, even if it's not Harry Potter."

#

Both me and Evan are deeply engaged in our international communities.

Obviously, it is a very difficult career to undertake for a writer who's not based in the USA, a Greek writer, and an Italian writer. With Evan's experience, I wanted his insight into how he thinks the industry can help to discover the future of storytellers who are not necessarily privileged. With us, we live in the States, but how would those writers get those shots?

"I think the festivals that read unproduced screenplays are critical. When you are an international writer, you better be sure that when you're writing in a language that is not your first language, you've mastered it completely. Otherwise, it's going to sound translated. And that's not a screenplay.

It's one thing to talk about unproduced writers in the US who absolutely need more venues for their material to get seen, as opposed to this torturous game of Russian Roulette, where you're trying to approach agents.

But you can't get an agent unless you get the sale and you can't get a sale without an agent. And don't forget, agents have only so much bandwidth to read a new writer's material, they've already got their clients and most of them have more clients and they know what to do with."

Unfortunately, it is true that these old boys' clubs are everywhere: in Italy, you couldn't get anything green-lit or sold or written unless it was done with a political message about the society and the culture. And it was very sort of art-house so it didn't really have a commercial value. And if it did, they would shut it down. They will not open the doors to those storytellers. Now, it's changed a lot, and I feel like Greece is changing a lot. We have so many movies that are candidates for Oscars nominations, I hope that there will be more people like Evan and me who will create groups that can foster those new voices, and show them how to Final Draft. And read Save the Cat by Blake Snyder.

"When I was at American University, one of our textbooks was Vicki King's "How to write a screenplay in 31 days.""

It is invaluable to me because I cannot tell you how many young writers I've met, who have been working on one script for the last two years.

And I recognize the quality of rewriting and rewriting and rewriting. But a part of getting hired in the film business is being fast and delivering within a very specific amount of time. Now, again, I don't work in television, but I think television is particularly fast. But even in features, you have to be able to hit your targets and turn things around quickly.

People appreciate speed. And that book taught me how to write fast. And I think a lot of my career has come out of the fact that I can turn things around quickly."

WRANGLING CATS
with JAY RUSSELL

"Learning to make films is very easy.
Learning what to make films about is very hard." George Lucas

With an MFA in screenwriting and directing from Columbia University, Jay Russell is a film director, producer, and writer and has written on projects for Paramount Pictures, Imagine Entertainment, and more. Known for his warm-hearted family movies, Jay has a knack for telling simple, straightforward tales with an earnest, emotional resonance.

In my talk with Jay, we explore his journey and the transition from traditional film to digital.

"It started as a kid, I went through all the different formats. I used to shoot on little Super 8, starting with the basics. When I got into college, I would shoot on 16 mm and then later on 35mm. A lot of kids now not only do not know about shooting on 35mm they much less about cutting it. In my first two movies, we actually sat at the table and used the knife and cut the picture, and that's how we edited it.

And then, though a lot of people were shooting digital already, I shot The Water Horse for Sony in New Zealand and Scotland, and I had the choice of shooting digital but I was still trying to stick to the idea of shooting on film. There are certain directors like Chris Nolan and Tarantino who still just absolutely want to shoot it on film. But on digital these days, the image quality is pretty much there now. There is a certain ease to it, you don't have to worry about the scratches happening on the negative and so forth. But of course, you do have to worry about something with the hard drive.

I can't tell you how many times there have been cases of shooting on film where we have a scene going and as we're shooting I might give a direction to an actor, and we try something else while the film is still rolling. And then you have the camera operator raise their hand as we're about to run out of the film. In digital, you can just keep shooting, plus there are definitely advantages in post-production but I still love the look of the film. Maybe before it's all over, I'll shoot something else on film. But it's a new world in production these days."

#

The advantage of shooting digitally is being in the video village and seeing what is going on, and you can go back and reshoot it if necessary. But I wanted to know why Jay wanted to be a director.

"For me growing up, it was more of a toss-up of two things that I really loved: I loved music, and I was a musician. But I also loved movies. In some of my earliest memories of going to the movies with my parents, they would take me to the old Disney Family Films with Dean Jones and Kurt Russell - those Disney comedies. And then the big blockbuster things like Sound of Music and I was overwhelmed by the big screen and having pictures tell a story.

Another thing, and you wouldn't know it by the movies I've made, I was also a big horror movie fan when I was a kid. I loved in particular the British horror movie with Christopher Lee and Peter Cushing. So my first little Super 8 movies were all just complete gorefest, all about blood and guts and stuff. In fact, one of the things I am working on now is a horror movie, because those are the movies that made me want to be a director in a weird way.

So as time went on, I just lost my interest in music. Music is sort of athletics, in that at a certain point you know whether you're going to be able to do it professionally or not. You know, whether you're going to be able to play basketball in the NBA. As a musician, you need to ask yourself: can I do this professionally? Am I good enough to be able to play either in a major Symphony or play jazz with a group?

While I was trying to figure out what am I going to do, I just spent more time in the theatre department at my college and started writing scripts. I got a lot of encouragement from one of my professors about a couple of scripts I'd written and then, it sort of went from there. And I just never looked back. "

#

I find it interesting that Jay's first movie was about a dog and then went on to films with children. I would think those are probably the hardest things to do when you are starting quote-unquote, as a director to direct animals and children.

"Well, even before Skip, I'd made a little a very small budget independent film even before that. You had mentioned in your intro, that I'd shot a lot of documentary stuff. So all of that was good training ground going into that the first quote, prominent film, which was Skip, and the training ground was with the documentaries, the training was thinking on your feet because if you're shooting things in real-time, and in reality, there is no take two, you know?

The other thing that I learned while I was shooting all that documentary work, was I would still cover scenes that were happening in real life. But if the drama was happening in front of me, I still would try to film it as you would a movie, with close-ups and trying to follow the action and so forth. But doing it on the fly was excellent training for being prepared for anything. And so when it came to with Skip, when it came to working with kids and animals, I had to be prepared for anything, because you know, as much, as well as a dog might be trained for a movie, or, maybe an experienced kid actor, you still never know what's going to happen, because one day the kid is tired, and he just can't, he's just not there. So you got to figure out a way to make it happen. And the same with a dog.

The funny thing with animals and film is most of the things they do, it's food-based, it's like if they walk from here to there, then they get a treat. Or if they run across a field, then they get a treat. Well, at a certain point, you know, they aren't hungry anymore. And then that's when it gets tricky when the treats don't mean anything to them.

But the key to that, and I think the key to all movies working was A) we had a really good script, and B), the actors. There was a great cast of actors, but they understood the complications of what we were doing. We had to wait for the dog to get hungry again. Or the kid needs to take a nap because he's cranky. So, it took a real sort of group effort to make that happen. And I was there to wrangle it all together."

\#

Directing to a great degree, it's like wrangling cats -because the cats run off in all different directions, you have to get them somehow in the same room together.

\#

I wanted to learn more about how it was working on a film like Ladder 49, dealing with big names like John Travolta and Joaquin Phoenix. Jay has been involved in his own projects as a writer and producer, I wanted to hear more about the transition from children, and family fare to something powerful, and emotionally impactful like Ladder 49. Which is a movie people still look at as one of the original movies about firefighters.

"Thanks, Alexia. To me, it's all about storytelling. You know, whether you're telling a story of a boy and his dog, or in the case of Tuck Everlasting, whether you're telling a story about a family who's immortal, or in the case of Ladder 49, these firefighters trying to save one of their own, which is when Joaquin's character gets trapped in a burning building, and then we look back over his life, it's all storytelling.

The wrinkle in Ladder 49 whereas with Skip the wrinkle was the dog, never knowing how exactly the dog is going to behave, in Ladder 49 it was the fire. All the fire that you see in the movie, it's all real. I mean, there was no- at the time we shot that digital work sophisticated enough to be able to put fire in those settings. So we had to have real fire all the time. The actors were highly trained in their jobs, which by the way ended up really working for the characters of the movie because they went to the Fire Academy, including Joaquin and Travolta. And so by the time we actually shot the film, they were practically trained well enough to work for the fire department, we had to do that because we were sticking them in the fire. And if something had gone wrong, which it could have, at any time, they had to know how to get themselves out of it, and how to save themselves. So it was, so that was the dog, and that movie was the fire, dangerous, and it had us all, you know, on edge all the time.

But if at the end of the day, though, it was just telling a story. And the rest of it was just a matter of putting the shots together. I'm gonna jump ahead for a second, but it's to your point, when I made this movie, the Waterhorse for Sony, it involved a ton of digital effects. I mean more digital effects than I've ever worked with, something like 1200.

I had a great conversation with this fella named Joe Letteri, who was our visual effects supervisor for that film. Joe is also the person who runs Weta Digital down in New Zealand for Peter Jackson. And Joe has a string of Oscars on his desk. He did all the Lord of the Rings movies, and he did King Kong with Peter and he did Jurassic Park, going back to Spielberg.

Joe is like the guru of visual effects and gave me the greatest tip I think I've ever gotten. When you're doing these visual effects movies, it might be easy to get overwhelmed with the scope of everything you're doing. And he said to me, one day, we're sitting on the set: you know, Jay, we make these things one shot at a time.

And that was just the most simple, but it just completely put me at ease. Because I stopped worrying about the hundreds and hundreds and hundreds of shots that I had to get with visual effects, it was just one shot at a time. And when you focus that way, well, then suddenly you are not overwhelmed. It was that similar approach to Ladder 49, which is Yeah, we're going to be doing a lot of crazy stuff in this. But it's one shot at a time, you know. "

#

Because I stopped worrying about the hundreds and hundreds and hundreds of shots that I had to get with visual effects, it was just one shot at a time. And when you focus that way, suddenly you are not overwhelmed.

#

Working on so many projects in different countries, under different circumstances - I wanted to know if he had any specific memory that stood out, or if he ever had the feeling of I've made one of my best works here, or even when a relationship with an actor where magic was happening.

"I love working with all the actors I've worked with, and I've had the great fortune of working with some really good ones in all the different movies and a lot of people who have Oscars on their desks. But working with Joaquin was special. Every single day was exciting because I haven't met and doubt that I ever will meet another actor who stays committed to his craft. He just never lets up.

There isn't a day where he's a little off. It's just not going to happen with him. And therefore, because he's so prepared and he's so committed, you have to show up with your A-game all the time. I think that was probably the most exciting experience I'd had with an actor but also one of the memorable things happening on a set was with him.

I was saying the fire was hazardous stuff, and no one got injured in the movie, not even a turn of an ankle. I mean, we were really lucky. However, there was one shot, one day, I'll never forget because it scared the crap out of me. Joaquin- it is at the beginning of the movie, if you see the movie, you'll see there's this big explosion, and this building, and the floor collapses underneath Joaquin and he slides down and falls a number of floors. Obviously, that was on a set, and the floor collapse was all a mechanical thing and where the floor would go at different stages.

But as he was sliding down, the floor collapsed, and all of this burning material fell but it was supposed to fall after he went down into the hole. But something happened, and there was some misfire, no pun intended, but when he slid all the fire came down right on top. And if you watch really closely in that sequence, you'll see that the jacket on his back is on fire. And you'll also see this one big chunk of flaming something land right by his face. I'm talking about inches from his face.

Another interesting thing about that is that was one of the last shots we did on the entire film. So we almost burned Joaquin up on the very last day of shooting. But fortunately he never even knew he was on fire. Because when he slides down into the hole, there were like three actual firefighters that just put him out immediately. And he didn't even know that he was on fire. But that was certainly a memorable moment.

The other one I can think of was only because it's a shot for people who liked the movie, that really moves people at the end of My Dog Skip. We have this scene where the old skip, this old dog is going to get up on the bed that he always would sleep on when his boy was a boy. And now he's grown. And at the very end of the movie, that dog goes to the bed, and he's trying to get up on it, as he always did. But he's too old and arthritic. So then Kevin Bacon has to pick him up and put him on the bed. Everybody just bawls their eyes out when at that scene. Well, that scene almost didn't happen. Because as I was talking about, you know, with dogs. Dogs can usually only do one trick or two tricks at a time because the rest of it is too confusing for them. And they know if I do the one trick, I'll get a treat. If I did the second trick, I'll get a treat. But that's about it. Well, in that shot, the dog had to do three or four things, it had to walk in this really slow sort of crippled way. And that's one trick. It had to get up to the bed and put its paw up on the bed, that's two tricks. Then it had to scratch as it could you know like it was trying to get up. That's three tricks. And then it had to turn around and look at Kevin Bacon when he was going to come and pick him up and put them on top of the bed. So it was like four or five tricks. And we almost didn't get it. I mean, we just kept shooting and shooting. And finally, the producer puts his hand on my back. And he goes: Yeah, Jay I don't know if this is going to work. Let's rethink it. And we're going to be here all day. So you got to move on.

And I said: can we just try one more time? Just one more time. And on that last time, he did it perfectly. It's just as you see in the movie. That's what happened on that very last shot.

So those are two kinds of big memories I have shooting."

#

As our conversation is wrapping up, I wanted to know if Jay had some words of advice he would like to give to anybody who is aspiring to be a filmmaker, television maker, or any type of content creator. And of course, if he had the most significant words of wisdom.

"I'm gonna throw two things out there. And one of them I'm going to steal from the fellow who said it to me, and I'll say it again: you make these things one shot at a time. Don't be overwhelmed by stuff.

The other thing is, and this may be the most important, and I talk to young filmmakers about it all the time: we all get anxious, and we want everything to happen all at once.

I tell them is, it's not a sprint, it's a marathon. And you have to be willing to go the distance. If it happens overnight, well, then hallelujah. But it almost never does. And it's a marathon."

#

If you're not ready to run the marathon, then don't get involved with it, because it's a long, long, and winding road - as the Beatles song says.

WITH AN OPEN HAND
with DEEDEE PFEIFFER.

"Fear is the number one emotion that we are spending tremendous amounts of brainpower to cover up" - Jodie Foster

Deedee Pfeiffer from the hit television series "Big Sky" has also starred opposite so many hotties in Hollywood: she worked with Michael Douglas, Keanu Reeves, George Clooney, and Jeff Goldblum. Then she took a 10-year hiatus to study psychology, how to be a social worker, and - she is an animal advocate. And for everyone who knows me, I am a fellow animal advocate. And she just went on a road trip, so, of course, I want to hear about this and what real life is for stars. I wanted to know how filming in New Mexico worked out when the show was set in Montana.

"I am so flattered and honored to talk with you. You know, in our first season of Big Sky, we were in Canada. We actually started in New Mexico, we were there for like a second. Covid happened, and we shut down and resurfaced in Canada. Now we are back in New Mexico. And yes - I did do a road trip with my 15-year-old son and my rescued rottweiler, my rescue cat, and my son's rescue cockatoo in a very teeny car!

It was supposed to be this amazing journey, we were going to bond, and it was nothing like that. I am still recuperating from the trauma of that 17-hour road trip!

Now I am back doing the second season, and it feels good. The first season I was in quarantine in Canada, feeding the Canadian pigeons and any bird I could get my hands on at the inner balcony. This time I got my own rugrats, and my animals here keep me busy.

When we first came to New Mexico, I thought it was kind of desert-y, and it is also very beautiful. But they found locations closer to the mountain area where it looks like Montana, so I guess they are doing their movie magic. I like what they do for me for the camera all the time.

I did see pictures where there's snow in New Mexico, which I'm so excited about because my son and I never had a snowy Christmas, I am looking forward to that.

I am really interested to see the cockatoo in the snow, I don't think Precious nor the rottweiler is going to like their little California paws in the snow so we'll see how it works out."

#

A lot of artists are entering into their artistic endeavors for three reasons. It is either passion, for purpose, or ambition. Sometimes it's a combination of all three. I wanted to know what the reason was for Deedee.

"I've been really fortunate. I've had two journeys - the first was when I was 18 to now that I am 57. I am one of those who actually admit that I am 57.

It was 10 years ago, at the age of 47 I took off for 10 years to get my education. For me, the first time it was curiosity and wanting to conquer something I'd never tried before, and I knew from the get-go that I

was really bad at it. The minute I went from acting class from 18 to 20, I was so bad. I was told Oh my god, why are you bothering with this? But I kind of had this hardheadedness, my dad used to call me a hard head, I wanted to figure it out first before I could quit or go on to something else. Well, now 30 years later, I still couldn't figure it out. Still trying to conquer it. Never really ever could, I don't think you ever can, as an artist, ever to figure it out.

You write on a daily basis on a moment-to-moment basis and as an artist, if you're not evolving and changing then you're missing the boat and you're stagnant.

And as you know, it is always breathing. It's its own entity and especially when I took 10 years off and I came back, now I am back sober. This month, I will be three years sober. It took a year off of my schooling to get my butt sober. I had to realize I was an addict and an alcoholic. So for me to now be acting again not only with my degrees but sober - it is a whole other journey.

I am not looking through the lens of fear anymore. I don't have as much insecurity. I'm always insecure, but not as much. My drive is just as important but my purpose is different. I want to bridge together my 10 years of education on social welfare issues when it comes to homelessness, mental health, and of course, addiction because that's me. I want to be an advocate to say Hey, let's talk about these things, let's talk about addiction. I would talk about anything else in my life. It shouldn't be this big monumental thing.

Deedee Pfeiffer had or has, as you know, an addiction. Yeah, I do. Yeah. Nice to meet you. And now let's have a conversation about it, right? So the more we normalize it and pull the shame away from it, the more we can get to those of us who carry a lot of shame as addicts.

So I love playing Denise in Big Sky because Cody clearly had an alcohol problem. So secretly I made Denise sober - no one knows that. I like coloring this character through my life journey, as a social worker, and as a Bachelor in Psych, made Denise kind of like her own little therapist, who is also sober. So she is a lot of things."

#

Once you think you have the answers, I think you're done as an artist because life is ever-changing.

#

DeeDee's rawness and authenticity are coming through on screen, and I wanted to explore more if this is something that came from COVID and everything everyone went through. I am curious about that as I often hear people talk about residual PTSD, and I think with everything happening today, people are feeling the need to open up that hidden box and show their demons and there is no longer shame attached to those demons. I wanted to know if that is one of the reasons DeeDee also was so open and unafraid, or if we had not gone through a pandemic would she not have been so open?

"There is a lot of truth there. But for me, I know that in my recovery as an addict, transparency is key to staying sober each day. Calling myself on my own shit, having supportive people around me that I make sure I don't have people around me who cosign my bullshit, right? So transparency is a big one. When I realized when I came out of rehab, and I was starting to admit it, I had a problem and now I'm no longer the identified problem in my family or friends. And it just gives me the chills. I want to let everybody out there know that if you have an issue with whatever you are addicted to - I don't care if it is gambling, sex, or heroin. Whatever - and addiction is an addiction. It carries a lot of shame. I get you, grab my heart, I get you! I still have shame. It is an ugly one, it kneecaps you. And yet you can do this if you just lean on somebody who's maybe got some sober legs ahead. I lean on people who have more years than me, and that is a big part of that is transparency. I started the journey of that three years ago.

COVID just brought it to another level. With COVID there's something else we don't talk about: Grief. During COVID, everybody was grieving our norms, on a lot of things. People had a lot of loss during COVID on all sorts of levels. So when one looks at one's grief, there are a lot of different stages of grief. And if we have compassion for each other and understand that it is going to take some time to get through it. You don't go around it like I did. You go around it, then you're not really going through it, and going through it sometimes means leaning into it. And grief has a lot of faces that aren't so pretty just like when you're in your disease.

But just like in recovery, getting through grief can also be part of saying: I want to be part of the solution, not the problem. And the way to do that is to say hey, it's okay to say this is frickin' hard. How about that? And it doesn't make me a weak person, it makes me an honest person. And if someone views me as weak, that's cool. That's the lens that they're looking at life through. I try daily to make sure the lens that I'm looking through is a lens that is hopefully not broken like it used to be.

And we can check our own lens and it's exciting. Every day I don't drink, every day I'm an identified possibility, showing other people that if I could do this, and I'm a hard head, you can do it too! I know it is hard, but you can do it, we can get through this grief, we can find what our new normal is - all this stuff."

#

I am now an identified possibility. How exciting is that?

#

Being raw and honest is important, as is being seen. I feel the pandemic was a major wake-up call because it allowed us to ask - what is really important? Is it the likes on Instagram, or being invited to premieres so you can show you are relevant or is it something else? I wanted to explore this more with DeeDee.

"A lot of people are telling me I need to get more followers on Instagram, I can do the dot or the check or whatever it is. Thank you for your concern, I am ok. I love the fact that people are following me discovering me or they've been fans for a while or whatever, or they think I'm quirky and fun. And they like my videos of birds, and I'm good. I don't need that check. I don't need that little dot saying I have a million followers. Actually to me, that is a little bit overwhelming. And surely not very intimate.

I'm intimate with the followers I have, I can click back and like what they post. But I think you hit on something when it says being heard, being seen. It is so hard to be seen or heard. If you don't have the skills to communicate or say what needs to be heard. That's where we can all become a little more savvy. For instance, teenagers, yelling all the time you don't hear me, you don't see me, you're not listening to me and all we do is look at the behavior. But if you look at the people's behavior, they're yelling and screaming. Usually, it's just not about the words. So communicating in certain ways - drinking is a way to communicate that I am slowly dying because of my undiagnosed trauma or whatever it is, or as a full-blown addiction. But when you say being seen first the person has to be able to verbally say Hey, see me. But often they are doing that without saying those words. We have to learn how to communicate in a different, richer, deeper way.

My kids are like Mom, Just stay in your lane. They're right! They are right and I'm all up in their lane because I'm the parent and you should let me stay in your lane. So now I'm like: Okay, well I'm over here in my own lane when you need me. I'm over here just, I love you over here - in my own lane."

#

Being seen is more important than being important.

#

Switching gears, I want to loop back to Big Sky. I was surprised to see David E. Kelley on the show. The show is so dark, and that is not his style. And with DeeDee's character on the show, where the character is living in a world of darkness- how is DeeDee keeping it together?

"A lot of people find the show dark. But they keep going, it's like an adequate crack - this is bad, but I'm going to keep looking. They want to see it, but you know what I love it is disguised as entertainment, but in the end, I really appreciate that there is always a message saying if you know

97

somebody in danger, if you know somebody who may be a victim of trafficking that is such a touchy subject and if we have to discuss it as you know, entertainment to bring awareness to very certain, very delicate things. I think that's a really great thing that David E. Kelley did.

As a recovering addict, one of the things I do is process how I'm feeling, and what I'm feeling with my sober group. My sisters are just fantastic. I bond with them on a different level.

My children, it's just getting back to putting my roots firmly in the ground. When I come home, all of that actor stuff goes away. Because when I come home, I have a bird clean up after, I have a dog that hasn't been walked, and a litter box that hasn't been cleaned. I got to start yelling at some boys: Why didn't you… All of a sudden I am now a real person with everyday issues that other parents have to deal with right. And then at the end of the day, I go Oh, yeah - how was my day at the set? And then I can reflect on it.

That is why I always say, please don't take it personally, but I don't watch my own interviews, and I don't listen to my own interviews. And I certainly don't watch my work to see if I'm making an ass of myself. I don't find it pleasant listening to myself or watching myself. But also, it's like it's done. It's in the universe now. It's behind me. There is nothing I can do to change it, other than maybe alter the next interview.

But I know that in each interview, like now, I'm coming from a place of my authentic self right now. And that is all I can give you in this interview. And I do that with all my interviews. So I am able to let it go.

And I do the same thing on set. I give the crew, the cast everything I got, and then I can let it go and then come home and give the rest to my animals and my sons, and I try to replenish DeeDee. I like watching shows on aliens."

#

I think what I've learned, the older I get is to be in the moment. Really just saturate myself in the moment and what's behind me in the past is gone.

#

I love watching shows on Aliens too, but I need to continue the talk with DeeDee about her journey. And I commend her for her authenticity in the show, and of course how can you say no to David E. Kelley?

But I want to know what she gravitates to as an artist. What will the new DeeDee 2.0 say yes to?

"As an actress, what makes you say yes to a part is because you've been out of the loop for 10 years. The new DeeDee 2.0, I love that. Some days it is 1.5. But that's ok. I will take any number. I definitely want to ride the show out for as long as it goes, I do have an idea of what I'd like to do next. I'd like to merge my education on social welfare issues on a micro level, through the lens of a social worker that I was taught through UCLA, which is a biopsychosocial lens. Pull those things together. And have some kind of a town hall show where we talk about social welfare issues, and I will be the host.

Because I just want to use my format as an actor, as an arena to bring people in to have conversations like we're doing right now. It is through conversations, I think that we get to a really important level of issues that I think everybody is concerned about or another. I mean, when you drive through any one of your towns right now, homelessness is pretty much everywhere. It is very hard.

Getting out from underneath is mental only, especially after the pandemic, when it comes to addiction and mental health issues. So throwing money at these problems is no longer, I feel acceptable but at the same time let's bring like-minded together in a multi-disciplinary factor. Because everybody's issue whether homelessness or mental health or substance is different. You have different traumas, different families, and different cultures. You know there are a lot of factors that go with each individual person. So for me, that's how I think we should be addressing a lot of these problems. And I'm not seeing a lot of people talking about it loudly, so I would like to be not loud in your face. And I'm kind of done with the blame game. What are we going to do right now? Let's all brainstorm. And wouldn't it be an exciting show to watch? To get the wheel going? Right? Let people solve problems instead of creating them. So important as a community."

#

Passion, Purpose, or Ambition. Why not put a purpose behind your passion, which for DeeDee is performing? But also making the world a better place, and making both, putting them in a nice little pretty package and creating something that people can put a flashlight on an issue that we are facing right now.

It is interesting as the times are changing, even for actresses. Michelle, DeeDee's sister and fellow actress has a different brand. DeeDee has a brand. DeeDee has always been funny, she is beautiful so that has been her lane for so many years. Now more roles are opening up for women to not just be pigeonholed into something. You can be dramatic, funny, sexy - you can be anything. It's not just a comedy actress. She is the leading lady who is going to go and have the romance thing, or this person is going to be a lawyer.

I wanted to know if DeeDee thinks the #MeToo movement has something to do with that change.

"I think the #MeToo movement definitely helped. A lot of good came out of that. Something needs to change, and if not - sometimes it needs to be broken. To go a different direction, right? That women, we're being used in a certain way in front of the screen and now let's see what's next.

I think that change is important, even though I'm not a big fan of change. I think one of the biggest lessons for me is to learn how to move with the change. Because when I resist it, when you look through when you go through life, like this resistance, look at how the life looks, the world looks like this. But when I go with curiosity, look at everything I see." DeeDee illustrates this last statement opening her hands.

#

Curiosity versus resistance

REFERENCE LIST

- Hook Point by Brendan Kane *(Chapter 3)*
- The Pomodoro Technique by Francesco Cirillo *(Chapter 2 and Chapter 5)*
- The 48 Laws of Power by Robert Greene (Chapter 7)
- Hello He Lied by Lynda Obst *(Chapter 9)*
- So You Wanna Be a Producer by Lawrence Turman *(Chapter 9)*
- Born to Win by Zig Ziglar *(Chapter 13)*
- How To Write a Screenplay in 31 Days by Vicki King *(Bonus Chapter: The Studio Writer)*

ABOUT THE AUTHOR

Alexia Melocchi is an accomplished entertainment industry professional with a long-proven track record of success within both the domestic and international arenas. A vital contributor to the LITTLE STUDIO FILMS brand, Alexia Melocchi 's footing in the Entertainment Industry began in the international marketplace in the 1990s, as both a sales agent and buyer's representative for eleven theatrical distributors. As a P.G.A producer with 30 credits, with she currently uses her professional relationships and expertise in screenplay development, film and television IP packaging, securing co-productions, and arranging for US and International Distribution for her clients' projects. A regular participant at most major Film and Television markets as well as Festivals around the world, Alexia Melocchi still pursues international acquisitions and uses a global film marketing approach for the Projects of her Clients as well as the films she is producing under the Little Studio Films banner. During her tenure as a Sales Agent, she sold more than 50 movies to profit on behalf of her producer clients and acquired more than 150 major Studio and Independent films on behalf of the Distributors she has ongoing relationships in Italy, Greece, Latin America, Spain, France, CIS, and the Middle East. She was behind the acquisitions of films such as PEPPERMINT, THE BOY 2, LA LA LAND, ANNA, NOW YOU SEE ME 2, BEAUTIFUL BOY, SHAUN THE SHEEP, and many more on behalf of her international distributor clients.

Alexia Melocchi is fluent in French, Greek, Italian, and Spanish and is also an Advisory Board Member of ITTV, the US platform ECOFLIX, and the Hanè Saga Storytelling Conference. She is frequently invited as an expert Panelist on the Global Entertainment Industry. She was invited to discuss her expertise at ITTV, SEE FEST, the LOS ANGELES GREEK FILM FESTIVAL, the NORTH HOLLYWOOD CINEFEST, three consecutive CANNES FILM FESTIVAL panels (hosted by the PGA, Stage 32 and the Producers Network) and WOMEN IN ENTERTAINMENT.

www.ingramcontent.com/pod-product-compliance
Lightning Source LLC
Chambersburg PA
CBHW060337130626
46553CB00003B/1032